The Wonderful
Hebrew
עִבְרִית
Alphabet 2
Workbook

TARVER ELITE PUBLISHING

The Rev. Dr. Tracey Tarver

Printed in the United States of America

First Printing, 2021

Follow Rev. Tracey Tarver on social media

Facebook: Pekudei Learning Center

Publishing Company: Tarver Elite Publishing

ISBN: 978-1-5136-8221-1

TABLE OF CONTENTS

IT IS FORBIDDEN TO READ YAHWEH'S WORD OR STUDY THE HEBREW SCRIPTURES WITHOUT PRAYING

BEFORE THE READING

Baruch Atah Adonai, elo-heinu melech ha-olam, asher bachar banu mi-kol ha-amim v'natan lanu et Torah-to. Baruch Atah Adonai, noten ha-Torah.

Blessed are You, Adonai our Yahweh, Ruler of the universe, who has chosen us from among all the nations, and given us the Torah. Blessed are You, Adonai, Provider of the Torah.

AFTER THE READING

Baruch Atah Adonai, elo-heinu melech ha-olam, asher natan lanu Torat emet, v'cha-yei olam nata b'tocheinu. Baruch Atah Adonai, noten ha-Torah.

Blessed are You, Adonai our Yahweh, Ruler of the universe, who has given us the Torah of truth, and implanted within us eternal life. Blessed are You, Adonai, Provider of the Torah.

Torah does not change with the times; Torah is changeless but it is always relevant to our changing society.

In volume one of The wonderful Hebrew Alphabet, we covered the first 7 letters of the Hebrew Alphabet from Aleph to Zayin.

The Hebrew alphabet is called the Aleph-beit.

In this book we will delve into the next 8 letters of the Hebrew alphabet from Chet to Nun including the final (sofit) form of those letters.

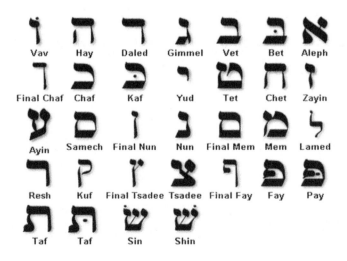

What is so important about the letters of Biblical Hebrew?

I was asked this question by a young Bible student. I answered him with the explanation that each letter has meanings on different levels. Letters make up words. The words make up the Bible and Yahshuah is the Living Word." As an added note, every letter IS A WORD in ITSELF.

Although he said, "interesting", the answer wasn't' sufficient for me. I pondered that questions afterwards, then I remembered that this young man was a nurse.

I may have given him a better answer by using a comparison. In the study of the human body, the first thing you must learn about is 'The Cell'. Cells make up tissue, tissue makes organs, organs make up the body which is covered by more cells, the skin.

This same principle can be related to every field of study. Whether it be science, where the root is and atom, or plants where the root is the seed, or light where the root is a ray, or sound, where the root is a wave, etc. If we want to study a particular thing or subject, we must start with the root system.

So it is with Biblical Hebrew. Since Yahweh SPOKE everything into existence, the first thing He created was

THE ALPH-BEIT. This is why Yahshua said "I AM THE ALEPH AND THE TAV. He did not say "I am the alpha and the omega". That is a Greek transliteration of the Hebrew Scriptures. So if you want to know Yahshuah, study the aleph-beit which is the foundation, the building blocks of creation. Yahweh has created His WORD great and glorious! We have the privilege to behold the awesomeness of His WORD by studying the individual letters which give HIS

MEANING to the words contained therein.

Many times, we will read a word and may think we understand the meaning. Although a Lexicon can be helpful, it's not until we study, search out, with much prayer, the individual letters of that word in Biblical HEBREW that we get Yahweh's TRUE meaning, which produces GROWTH and UNDERSTANDING.

Yahweh gave the language of BIBLICAL HEBREW to Adam, who thereby named all the animals. Adam was able to see the character of each animal and combine the Hebrew Letters from the Aleph-Beit to NAME each animal.

Thus, the reason why the serpent was able to tempt Eve. Unable to TWIST the words of Yahweh to Adam, he TWISTED the Words of Yahweh to Eve with "Did Yahweh Say?" He still works this same way today. He will tempt us by twisting the Words of Yahweh and say to us … "Did Yahweh Say?"

When we "Study to show ourselves approved by Yahweh", and gain a true understanding of His Word by learning the individual letters of the Aleph-beit, we are not so easily deceived. For how are we able to "Study the Word" without studying the "Letters?"

TAKE INTO YOUR HEART THAT THE LETTERS ARE OF THE UTMOST IMPORTANCE!

THE TORAH WAS OFFERED TO THE NATIONS

In a Midrashic account… Lest the nations of the World complain that Yahweh was unfair in not offering the Torah to the rest of the world, Yahweh did in fact offer it to all the other nations of the world and was turned down by all. **When the scriptures mention the other nations of the world, it is referring to the known nations as groups of people.**

Yahweh first offered it to the descendants of Esau, who lived near Mt. Seir, in accordance with the inheritance that Yahweh had given them. **Yahweh gave them that portion of the land.** When he offered them the Torah, they asked, "What are its laws?" When Yahweh told them that one of its laws was "You shall not murder," they said, "How can we accept the Torah? That law goes against our very nature, as Isaac said to our father, Esau, "And you will live by the Sword!" (Genesis 27:40)

He next offered it to Amon and Moab, who likewise turned it down. They asked, "What are the laws of the Torah?" When they heard that immorality was one of its main prohibitions, they said, "Our national origins are bound up with a story of immorality between Lot's daughters and their sleeping father. (Genesis19:30-38) Immorality has become part and parcel of our national character.

When he offered it to the descendants of Ishmael, they could not then, and they cannot now, deal with the prohibition against stealing (Vayikra 19:11), as the Angel of Yahweh said to our mother Hagar about our ancestor, Ishmael, "He will be a person without self-control, with his hand in everyone else's property, and everyone else's hand in his property, and he will camp on the borders of everyone else's land." (Genesis 15:12)

It was only when He offered the Torah to the Hebrew People that He found a Nation with the potential and willingness to live according to all the laws of the Torah. And they realized this potential by saying to Yahweh, "Naaseh V'nishma, **"We will first obey, and then understand,"** (Exodus 23:7), when He offered them His Holy Torah. **In other words, We won't ask first but we will obey first even when we don't understand. How many of us are willing to do that today? To obey first, even when we don't understand? – MIDRASH**

Blessed is Yahweh our God, King of the universe, who had chosen us from among all the peoples of the world and has given us His Holy Word. **(Annotated)**

SOUND THE SHOFAR!

The Holy Day of Shavuot (Pentecost) is in commemoration of the giving of the Torah on Mt. Sinai.

The entire people heard the words of Yahweh, and they became frightened.

They begged Moses to be the intermediary between Yahweh and them, for if Yahweh Himself would continue to give them the entire Torah, they would surely die. Moses told them not to be afraid, for Yahweh had revealed Himself to them so that they would fear Him and not sin.

Then Yahweh asked Moses to ascend the mountain; for he alone was able to stand in the presence of Yahweh. There Moses was to receive **the two tablets containing the Ten Commandments and the entire Torah,** to teach it to the children of Israel. Ever wonder why Yahweh gave the Ten Commandments on **TWO TABLETS INSTEAD OF ONE? READ ON...**

Moses went up the mountain and stayed there forty days and forty nights, without food or sleep, for he had become like an angel. During this time, Yahweh revealed to Moses the entire Torah, with all its laws and the interpretations thereof.

Finally, Yahweh gave Moses the two stone Tables of Testimony, containing the

Ten Commandments, written by Yahweh Himself.

Why did Yahweh write the 10 commandments on two tablets instead of one?

One reason is because they relate to each other. In other words, #1 relates to #6, #2 relates to #7, #3 relates to #8 , #4 relates to #9 and #5 relates to #10! Take time to notice the relevance of the commandments. The first Commandment is to Love the Lord with all your heart and soul, the sixth commandment is thou shall not murder. The relevance? Man is made in the image of God, so to murder would be to disregard the sanctity of man. By aligning the commandments in this way you will be able to see how they relate to one another.

"You gave us, Yahweh our God, the Torah of life and loving-kindness, righteousness, blessing, mercy, life and peace. Open my heart to Your Torah, and let my soul eagerly pursue Your commandments."

There will be commandments that you don't understand, never-the-less, take into your heart to first **obey** and then **understand.**

Notes:_____

_____

_____

_____

_____

_____

_____

_____

_____

CHAPTER 1

CHET 8TH LETTER OF THE HEBREW ALPHABET

In classical Hebrew script, the graphic design of CHET is formed using the two letters that precede it, the VAV AND the ZAYIN. CHET is an upside down "V" with a thin line (a yoke or bridge) that connects the Vav and Zayin. *On top of the vav and zayin is a chatoteres, a bridge that unites the two. The VAV can present the male principle, the husband. The Zayin can represent the female principle, the wife. The bridge that links them together is Yahweh. The Maggid of Mezritch better explains the verse "The woman of valor is the crown of her husband" as: the zayin, the crown, can represent the position of the woman of valor safeguarding the man.*

Chet and Hei

CHET looks like HEI, but HEI has a WINDOW. CHET has no WINDOWS. The only way to go is UP or DOWN THERE IS NO OTHER ESCAPE!

HEI has an airy sound, breathing out but CHET has a guttural sound in the back of the throat. HEI CAN BE SYMBOLIC OF THE BREATH OF GOD

LOOKING AT CHET IN MARRIAGE

The VAV represents the male and the ZAYIN represents the female and is representative of the male and the female coming together under the marriage canopy, the CHUPPA which is the first meaning of the letter chet. There are three partners in marriage, Man, woman, and God. The VAV, represents the male, ZAYIN, represents the female and the upside down "V" repesents Yahweh who is above all and brings His covenant and peace into the home.

Isiah 30:31 states that "At the voice of Yahweh Assyria will be devastated" The letter CHET can also mean "The Fear of Yahweh" or "The Voice of Yahweh" and alludes to "Destruction, devastation and fear".

This is when you have the male and female without the presence of Yahweh. The marriage will be devastating. In marriage a husband is not allowed to abuse his wife with words because tears flow freely from women and if a woman is made to cry swift retribution will come upon the individual. So, husbands are warned to respect their wives and not treat them harshly in order to be rich because wealth in the marriage is at the merit of the woman. Further instruction is given in the New Testament where God admonishes for husbands to love their wives Ephesians chapter 5. **(Annotated)**

So this is the CHET on one hand it can be love and peace on the other hand it would be devastation.

The Talmud tells us that if man and woman, איש ואשה (ish v'isha), are meritorious, the Divine presence will rest between them. The word ish, man, is spelled איש, alef, yud, shin. Isha, אשה, woman, is spelled alef, shin, hei. In both ish and isha we find the letters alef and shin. Alef and shin spell eish, the Hebrew word for FIRE! The fire that exists between man and woman fuels a fiery, passionate relationship. But if there were only this flame igniting the marriage, the fire of passion CAN all too easily be changed into a **fire of destruction**. Yahweh must also be in the marriage, and fortunately He is: the YOD of the ish, in the name of the man, when combined with the hei of the isha, the name for the woman, give us the very name of Yahweh. YOD -HEI-VAV-HEI, THE TETRAGAMATRON. Vav has a gematria of 6 and Zayin has the gematria of 7; 6+7=13 which is the same number of AHAVA meaning Love. That is the purpose of Marriage between a husband and wife. The gematria of EHUD is 1, " And the two shall become ONE flesh" Genisis 2:24; Matthew 19:5; Mark 10:8; Ephesians 5:31 **(Annotated)**

CHET AND UNDERSTANDING COMMUNITY

Vav can represent man individually or people and Zayin represents time where we get the Hebrew word for time (ZAYIN, MEM, FINAL NUN) TZIM. So, Vav and Zayin together can represent spending time with people which is our word for community or people in common unity = chavurah. **(Annotated)**

CHET AND THE COVENANT

The number 8 is associated with circumcision which is performed on the 8th day. **IT IS AMAZING THAT YAHWEH CHOSE THE 8TH DAY FOR CIRCUMCISION, WHEN VITAMIN K, THE CLOTTING AGENT IN THE BLOOD IS HIGHER IN A MALE THAT ANY OTHER TIME IN LIFE.** Also the harp of the Messiah will be reveal the 8th musical note. There are only 7 known notes in the musical scale. When Messiah comes, the 8th note will be revealed.

What is the similarity between the circumcision and marriage? Both are covenants. Circumcision is a covenant between Yahweh and His People and Marriage is a covenant between a husband and wife, A PROMISE.

This covenant says "Let us make a bond between the two of us so that we will always be together because there may come a time when we are not too interested in being together and this bond, this promise, this covenant will tie us together and even though we will go thru difficult times together we will have the strength to endure ONE ANOTHER AND THE ABILITY TO EVER REMAIN ECHUD {1}. THERE'S THAT UNITY OF LOVE AGAIN.

We have a covenant with Yahweh and Yahweh has a covenant with us. Regardless of the hardships, Yahweh promises that He will never forsake us. We have a covenant with Yahweh that we will serve Him as Yahweh and Keep His Commandments. Yahshuah said in John 14:15 "If you love me you will keep my commandments." **Love involves commitment and endurance**

Although we will endure hard times and fall short of Yahweh's Glory, we have righteousness thru the shed blood of Yahshuah and we will have times when we think we cannot hold on any longer, Yet again Yahshuah says in John 10:27-30 "My sheep hear my voice and I know them, and they follow me. And I give unto them eternal life and they shall never perish, neither shall any man pluck them out of my hand. My Father which gave them me is greater than all and no man is able to pluck them out of my Father's hand. I and my Father are one. When we face times that we think we can no longer hold on, remember the words of Yahshuah that strengthens us "In the world you will have trouble. But take heart! I have overcome the world. - John 16:33 NIV

Furthermore, Yahweh has a covenant with us that He will protect us and provide for us and give us good health and long life and give us eternal life. Yahweh like the Husband protects the wife. But sometimes Yahweh doesn't do what we expected. **Sometimes we don't have good health or wealth or long life. Does that mean that Yahweh has not kept His covenant? NO it doesn't. Yahweh has PURPOSE in EVERYTHING!** Yet, we still keep our covenant with Yahweh and He still keeps his covenant with us, even when we don't understand His purpose in things. I once seen a bumper sticker that read "The journey may get bumpy but you are promised a safe arrival."

Chet also has a pictorial design of a 'wall or fence'. When you think about a wall or a fence, the thought of protection and boundaries come to mind. Through the Chet, Yahweh gives us boundaries for our protection. That's what COMMANDMENTS are principles for our protection.

CHET AND LIFE

Several words relating to LIFE begin with the letter CHET

- Chayim   Life

- Chayah   Living

- Grace   Chen

To experience true life one must possess:

- Devotion   Chasidut

- Wisdom   Chokhmah

CHET AND NEW BEGINNINGS

8 is the number of new beginnings.

- 7 is completeness... 8 is a new beginning.

- Yahshuah rose from the grave on the **8**[th] day (the first day of the week.)

- Yahweh reaffirmed His covenant with Abraham **8** times.

- Yahshuah was born during the **8** day festival of Sukkot (The feast of Tabernacles) He tabernacle among us.

- David was the **8**[th] son of Jesse.

- Methuselah was the **8**[th] generation of man.

- Noah had 8 souls on the Ark that were saved during the flood.

- The process to cleanse a Leper or a Nazarite who was defiled was 7 days of purification and on the **8**[th] day the cleansing was complete.

8 IS A PICTURE OF YAHWEH AND YAHSHUA AND A NEW HEAVEN AND A NEW EARTH THAT WILL NEVER END

THE COUNTERFIET EIGHT

(Taken from Mark Mickelson 2013 - Annotated)

There is a counterfeit use of the number eight by Satan. In the end of this age, the false religion of Babylon described in Revelation 17 portrays Satan ruling over the earth before Yahshuah's return. The religions of Babylon have never passed away, they only changed disguises. Almost all of the secular "holy-days" have their roots in Babylon and Nimrod and Semiramis, His MOTHER/WIFE. Many of the images held by the Roman Catholic Church as symbols of Mary and baby Jesus is none other than Semiramis and her HUSBAND/SON Tammuz (Nimrod). To show that this false system had lived on and crept into the church, Yahweh gives a vision in the book of Ezekiel of the "women weeping for Tammuz". Ezekiel 8:13-15

The passage in Revelation describes seven kings: "They are also seven kings... The beast who once was, and now is not, is an eighth king. He belongs to the seven and is going to his destruction" (Revelation 17:10-11, New International Version). That false religious system of Babylon is the eighth of those kings.

The pollution of Christianity that came from Gnosticism (among other things) honored the number eight. One of the first false epistles, called the Epistle of Barnabas, argued on behalf of the eighth day and its importance. This false reverence of the number eight is what led to Sunday worship in Christianity by the Catholic Church. Yahweh blessed the SEVENTH DAY and mad it HOLY.

Samuel Bacchiocchi's book Sabbath to Sunday describes the Epistle of Barnabas, noting that the first and primary argument for the change from Sabbath to Sunday was the number eight. Next was the argument that Yahshuah rose on Sunday, first day of the week, which would be THE EIGTH DAY. Many people believe this is the reason for the change from the seventh day to the first or eight day. Later, Jerome argued that the number seven represented Judaism and the law, and the eighth day represented the gospel, so therefore, he argued, Christians must do away with the law. **(Annotated)**

CHET AND PRAYER

This is where we need to be very careful and exercise some discernment. With everything that was mentioned above about the 'counterfeit eight', we can see why it can be an image of a fence or a wall. We need to have the wisdom to see the boundaries. It's easy to see the good of the eight and very easily cross the line into the bad of it. This is where prayer, and much prayer comes into play.

Everything in the world of time revolves around the number seven: the seven days of the week the seventh year being a Sabbatical year, the observance of a **Hakhel** year every seven years. Eight, however, represents transcendence, a level that is beyond the natural order. When we go beyond the natural order of things and transcend the limitations put into place by Yahweh, we are vulnerable.

About the letter CHET, the Jewish commentary says:

"GOING BEYOND SEVEN, THE EIGHT SYMBOLIZES MAN'S ABILITY TO TRANSCEND THE LIMITATIONSOF PHYSICAL EXISTENCE. Thus, with a gematria or numerical value of eight, CHET stand for that which is on a plane above nature, i.e., the metaphysical Divine"

Let's look at the relationship between the Hebrew symbolism and the activity found in Revelation 8:1.

"And when he had opened the seventh seal, there was silence in heaven about the space of half an hour."

The scene has shifted to Heaven" on a plane above nature" where we see seven angels and seven trumpets. Everyone breathlessly awaits the next event. Then, another (the eight) angel arrives with a golden censer. He receives incense to offer along with **the prayer of the saints**. His censer is then cast to the earth, initiating yet another set of seven judgements. In this chapter, the judgements of Yahweh are linked with the incense of prayer. Here, we are reminded that it is through prayer that man transcends the limitations of physical existence. We communicate thru number 8 CHET, but we tread CAREFULLY. Keep in mind that prayer centers around our privilege to communicate with the Most High God and that must always remain our focus. Never allow that transcendence to take you to a place of mysticism involving human meditation and mantras. **(Annotated)**

CHET AND THE BLOOD OF YAHSHUAH

CHET is also an image of a door or a gate.

Speaking of His Word, Yahweh says:

And thou shalt bind them for a sign upon thine hand, and they shall be as frontlets (reminders) between thine eyes. And thou shalt write them upon the door posts of thy house, and on thy gates.

Deuteronomy 6:4-9

This is why we affix a MEZUZAH to our homes

Think of it as Yahweh's security system unless the LORD builds the house, its builders labor in vain. **Unless the LORD** watches over the city, the watchmen stand guard in vain. In vain you rise early and stay up late, toiling for food to eat - for he grants sleep to those he loves.

A mezuzah (Hebrew: "doorpost") represents the dividing line between the inside of a Jewish home or business and the outside world. Each mezuzah contains a rolled kosher parchment with the Shema prayer meant to protect the inhabitants. The case that holds the scroll can be simple or decorative, but the mezuzah itself is a reminder of your covenant with Yahweh. By obtaining the right material and hanging the mezuzah in the proper way, you can represent yourself with this symbol of our faith in YAHWEH, thereby obeying a commandment. Why did Yahweh command us to hang a Mezzuzah? Why a commandment to bind the words to your hands and let them be reminders between your eyes? As a safeguard. Yahweh has put in place reminders to help His people keep His commandments. We have yearly reminders in the way of Holy Days, We have a weekly reminder by way of the Shabbat, we have daily reminders of the tefillin, and tzit tzit and mezuzah, and we have a minute reminder through The Holy Spirit that dwells within us, and we have a reminder every second of our life as we are covered by 'The blood of the Yahshuah, the lamb of God. If we keep reminders in place and follow them, we can go from grace to grace in Him and not stray beyond " the fence or the wall' This is CHET.

The Israelites were instructed by Yahweh to put the BLOOD OF THE LAMB on the doorpost of their homes and to **STAY IN THE HOUSE** and the Death Angel would **PASS OVER**. That Blood was symbolic of the Blood of Yahshuah and the covenant of the New Testament in His Blood. Likewise, He also took the cup after **supper**, saying, "This cup is the new covenant in My blood, which is shed for you. (Luke 22:20)

We must **STAY UNDER THE BLOOD** and Death will not have a **sting** or the grave have **a victory.**

O death, where is thy sting? O grave, where is thy victory? 1 Corinthians 15:55

CHAPTER 2

TET

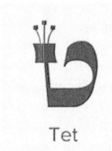

Tet

      The **ninth letter** of the Hebrew alphabet is called "Tet" (rhymes with "mate") and has the sound of "t" as in "tall".

The Hebrew letter Tet is shaped like a vessel that contains something good and hides it within. The first time the Hebrew letter Tet appears in the book of Genesis is in the word tov, "good," and hints to the highest form of divine love. Although we always refer to Moses by the name of Moses, His Hebrew name was "Tov" because his parents looked at him and realized that He was a 'goodly' child. Exodus 2:1-10

And Yahweh Saw That It Was Good

When we read that Yahweh "saw it was tov ('good')" following each day of creation, we should ask ourselves, what was this goodness that Yahweh saw? Everything that Yahweh created was perfectly designed to fulfill a particularly designed purpose. Every animal has the physical characteristics and abilities to sustain itself in their particular environment, to reproduce and defend itself. And so it is with Mankind. We are perfectly designed. As individuals we are to fulfill our divine purpose even when we don't understand what that purpose is, or we deny it. As long as we are in our own environment, we are designed to sustain ourselves, to reproduce and to defend ourselves. Most importantly, we are designed to Praise the Almighty God, this is our divine purpose. Everything that Yahweh created appeared so perfect completed so that on the seventh day Yahweh ceased from all the work that he had been creating and stood afar, like an artist, and declared: "it is VERY good." **(Annotated)**

HE IS GOOD

As we meditate on the letter TET we should burst into Praise! Yahweh gave us the example of what we are to do in His world in the first chapter of Genesis. When we see the beauty and awesomeness of the oceans and the seas, we should say **"He is Good"**. When we see the flowers and the trees, we should say, **"He is Good!"** When we see the sun, and the moon and the stars in the sky, we should say **"He is Good!"** When we wonder at the amazing fish in the sea and the beautiful birds in the sky, we should proclaim **"He is Good!"** When we see all the animals that are upon the earth we should declare, **"He is Good!"** but above them all, when we see another man or another woman, we should look for the **GOOD** in them and not focus on the bad. We should stand in awe of the Almighty and His greatest creation, that He chose to make in His image, that gives wisdom for them to be doctors, and astronauts, and scientist, and parents, and writers, and most of all obedient servants. And with every breath we should think upon the TET and resound, **"He is Good, He is Good, Yes He is VERY Good!"**

The letter Tet refers to the idea of noticing hidden blessings even in unpleasant events. As hard as it is to always maintain an optimistic perspective, we must accept any given situation, especially those that are difficult, with the belief that their hidden good is beyond our understanding. There comes a time when we must act in faith, regardless of what the situation looks like. We have just a limited frame of reference, we cannot see around the corner of time and space. We just can't see the whole picture. If we could only see the whole picture, then the particular situation that we face would make sense and indicates God's goodness and His perfect love for us.

The letter Tet is a letter of all the goodness in the world and how much goodness is hidden all around us, how the form of an object is hidden in the matter, how the soul is hidden in within the body, and how God is hidden in the world. God hides himself in creation so that we would have free will. If God were present, standing right in front of us, it would greatly influence our willingness to truly act as we desire in our hearts. Think of a child who does differently when their parents are at home opposed to their true behavior that comes out when the parent is not at home. Would we really do some of the things we do if God were RIGHT THERE??? The answer is a resounding NO! Therefore, God hides himself in creation, so that we will act in accordance with our free will. By doing so, it is clear to see if our actions are truly coming from the heart.

Tet's essence is feminine, representing the number 9 for the 9 months of pregnancy, and shaped like a womb, a spiral, a container where things change and transform. Just as we do not understand how bones grow in the womb, likewise we don't understand the mysteries of what goes on inside the TET. The infinite is contained in Tet and it brings about the finite.

The Tet contains the Hesed (kindness and mercy) of creation. It teaches us to distinguish between the good and the bad, and by choosing the good, we thereby to do that which is impossible, to erase the bad deed that was done. To change things around. *It contains the principle that nothing is lost, nothing is*

wasted, and all is eternal. The Tet is the container that creates the ability of Tikkun – that all souls are attracted to life with one purpose – to restore all to good as at the beginning. Tikkun means to fix or repair the world, to restore things to what they were when God created them....very good.

Consider that the summing the digits of the numbers represented by the **Hebrew letters** of the name "Adam" (אדם), results in the number nine. **Nine** is called the **mispar katan** (literally, "small number") of Adam, which alludes to the essential quality of man:

    א = 1

    ד = 4

    מ = 40

    Total: 9 (add the 1+4+4=9)

Unbelievably, we find that any **number times nine** equals nine (18, 27, 36, 45, 54, 63 etc), in mispar katan. 18 is 1+8=9, 27 is 2+7=9 etc. **(Proverbs) 12:19** *The lip of truth (Emet) shall be established for ever; but a lying tongue is but for a moment.*

Emet, truth, lasts forever. Therefore every multiple of nine remains a nine. Truth always remains the same and can never be altered. Similarly, Yahweh is true from beginning to end. Yahshuah stated " I am the way THE TRUTH, and the life" John 14:6

Adam is also in *mispar katan gematira* nine, for he alone from the entire universe was **graced** with the seal of truth from his Creator.

Psalms 8 says Adam was crowned with glory and honour Which could be interpreted as **tefillin** (which are imprinted with the Shin)--convert the word "Shin" to its mispar katan and you also get nine! (shin=300 yud=10 nun=50 combined sum is 360 = sum of the digits is 9! 3+6+0=9). Truth, emet=441 sum of

digits is nine! **(Annotated)**

According to Jewish law, once something is done three times it is considered a permanent thing. This is called a chazakah. Chazakah is established when an event repeats itself three times. This may be where the saying comes from, "The third time is a charm"! Once we have done something three times, we have connected to it and connected it to this world. "A three-fold cord is not easily broken" Ecclesiastes 4:12

Nine is three times three! **(Annotated)**

Hebrew letters with crowns

Tet is sometimes written with a crown on top

There is a famous story about tagin, told of the third-generation tanna Rabbi Akiva. *Rabbi Akiva was a leading Jewish scholar born 50 A.D. Died 135 A.D.*

When Moses ascended Mount Sinai to receive the Torah, he found God tying crowns onto the letters.

"God," said Moses, "surely you don't need those?"

God replied: "After many generations, there will be a sage named R' Akiva, who will derive heaps and heaps of halakhot (Laws and ordinances...ways) from them."

Taken from the Jewish Encyclopedia:

The significance of the tagin is veiled in the mysticism of the Cabala. Every stroke or sign is a symbol revealing, in connection with the letters and words, the great secrets and mysteries of the universe. The letters with the tagin are supposed, when combined, to form the divine names by which heaven and earth were created, and which still furnish the key to the creative power and the revelation of future events. These combinations, like the Tetragrammaton, were sometimes misused by unscrupulous scholars, especially among the Essenes. Hence, perhaps, the injunction of Hillel: "He who makes a common use of the crown [taga] of the Torah shall waste away" (Ab. iv. 7); to which is added, "because one who uses the Shem ha-Meforash has no share in the world to come" (Ab. R. N. xii., end); the words of Hillel, however, may be interpreted figuratively (Meg. 28b).

A plausible explanation of the tagin is that they are scribal flourishes, "iṭṭur soferim" (decoration of the scribes), the intention being to ornament the scroll of the Law with a "keter Torah" (crown of the Law), for which purpose the letters **ו, ג, ט, ע, ש, צ, ג** were chosen because they are the only letters that have the necessary bars on top to receive the tagin, excepting the letter "waw," of which the top is very narrow, and the "YOD," whose head is turned aside and has a point ("ḳoẕ") on the bottom. The tagin of the other letters were intended probably to serve as diacritical points for distinguishing between **ב** and **כ**, **ה** and **ח**, **ד** and **ר**, **ו** and **ז**, **ם** and **מ** wherever a mistake was possible. Technically, as noted above, a taga is composed of three ziyyunin, or daggers. A line or stroke placed on a letter with a flat top is called "ḳeren" (= "horn"), but as a rule authors are not careful to discriminate between the terms "horn" and "dagger."

Notes:_____

_____

_____

_____

_____

God spoke to Moses, and said to him, I am YHVH. I appeared to Abraham, Isaac, and Jacob as El-Shaddai, but by my name YHVH I was not known to them.

That second YHVH looks like this, in some traditions:

Three tagin per hei. This doesn't happen on all heys, nor yet on all instances of YHVH–just on certain ones. Why?

One scholar explains: There are tagin on the Name to indicate that this is the crowned, distinguished Name, the superior, explicit Name. And why on the heis specifically? Twice hei is ten, **and ten are the modes of existence:** (1) Utter height, (2) utter lowness, (3) utter east, (4) utter west, (5) utter north, (6) utter south, (7) utter good, (8) utter bad, (9) utter firstness, (10) utter lastness. **We are either up or down, east or west, north or south, good or bad, first or last. All that is in between may be considered pointless as we go in that direction. (Annotated)**

There is a second meaning to the letter TET, whose numerical value is 9, which can be seen by looking at Revelation Chapter 9. Isn't that ironic?

In Chapter 9, we are told of the blowing of the fifth and sixth judgement trumpets. The first trumpet gives us an image of a hoard of tormenting demons from the underworld. The second trumpet shows an army or 200 million "horsemen" whose work is to torment unrighteous mankind. It is clear to see the work of "that old serpent", the Devil in this chapter. The very shape of TET give the appearance of a snake with its head rising on the left and its tail coiling in on the right. ם (chabad.org)

Revelation 9:19 describes the torments that will afflict the world:

"For their power is in their mouth, and in their tails: for their tails were like unto serpents, and had heads, and with them they do hurt"

TET IS AN ENIGMA. MEANING BEING GOOD AND THE OTHER MEANING A SERPENT WHICH IS BAD

The rabbinic commentary clarifies the view:

"Man longs for a 'good' life, 'good' health, 'good' business, a 'good' year. But what is good? Success is often ephemeral (only lasting a short time) and prosperity corrupting, while setbacks and adversity often set the stage for advancement and triumph. Only God know what is truly, objectively GOOD for man" (Annotated)

In this chapter then, we see the sting of the serpent, tempered by the knowledge that behind all this horror is the objective goodness of Yahweh, as He uses these events to purify His people. It is also significant that the letter ט TET is said by the rabbis to represent diminishment followed by enlargement. In like manner the Tribulation will be followed by the Millennial reign of the Messiah. -CHABAD.ORG

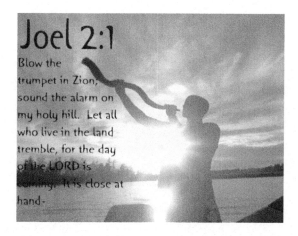

Joel 2:1

Blow the trumpet in Zion, sound the alarm on my holy hill. Let all who live in the land tremble, for the day of the LORD is coming. It is close at hand-

CHAPTER 3

YOD

The YOD is suspended in mid-air, and is the smallest letter in the Hebrew Alphabet, yet all the letters contain part of the YOD.

YOD represents a hand. Since all the letters of the Hebrew alphabet begin or end with the YOD, and since the YOD is the image of a "hand," you are able to see the HAND OF YAHWEH in each letter, either at the beginning or at the end of the letter.

Yahshuah upholds the world by the power of His Word (Heb 1:3), therefore, YOD is part of every letter and every word. YOD is considered the starting point and Yahweh is the starting point in everything.

YOD represents HUMILITY and has a knot that is vital and points upward to God. Since, again, YOD is part of every Hebrew letter, without the knot the entire Torah would be invalid.

Yahweh loves using the weak, small and humble. By using the little YOD to perform such a great work it shines forth His Glory and Wisdom.

Numbers 12:3 states that Moses was the most humble man on the face of the earth. This is seen when the word is read in Hebrew, for the word describing Moses as humble 'ana = humble', has an extra YOD (Annotated)

YOD has a numerical value of 10.

According to the Jewish sages, the **YOD** represents the world to come and completeness. The **YOD** is the most frequently used letter in the Aleph-Bet, as it appears in Hebrew texts approximately 11% of all the letters. This letter is unique in its appearance. It is the smallest letter of the Aleph-Bet and is therefore considered to be "modest." It also symbolizes wisdom, and it illustrates this by being small, like the small quantity of **truly wise individuals.**

According to the Talmud (the central text of Rabbinic Judaism), the letter **YOD** wanted to be the first letter of the Aleph-Bet. It asked this of the Creator of the world but was turned down. The Creator then comforted the letter **YOD**, with the fact that it is the first letter of His name, and even appears twice in the divine name. Since the **YOD** is so small, it also represents the super-natural, the things that are above the physical dimension.

The letter **YOD** is used in the Hebrew expression: **יוֹד שֶׁל קוֹצוֹ** (*kotzo shel YOD*). Literally translated as **the smallest edge of the letter YOD.** This expression is used to refer to something tiny, insignificant, or inconsequential.

It is interesting to note, that in most sacred literature, the pages are marked with letters, instead of numbers. (There are some books that use both formats.) When they get to the number 15, which would be the letters "**ה-י**," the printers avoid using this letter combination, since it is also one of the names of the Almighty. It is customary to instead use the letters **ט"ו** (numerical value 9+6 also equal to 15). Similarly, in the Jewish calendar, the 15th day of a month will be called **ט"ו** and not **ה-י**.

10 is significant in Torah, creation, the world, and the world to come.

- It took 10 generations from Adam to Noah to complete the breakdown of morality to such an extent that mankind-except for Noah and his family- had to be destroyed.

- 10 Generations from Noah to Abraham.

- It is said that with 10 utterances Yahweh created the world.

- There are 10 commandments (actually 613 commandments but they are summed up in the 10 commandments.)

- There were 10 plagues on Egypt that freed the Israelites.

- There are 10 Sefirot or emanations of Yahweh.

- Yahshuah spoke 10 "I AM" statements in the Gospel of John.

- Also in Hebrew, the name of Yahweh, Yahshuah, and Yisrael, Yerusalem all begin with the letter YOD, as well as the **TETRAGAMMATRON**, WHICH IS PICTURED BELOW

In Revelation chapter 10, the hand is a prominent part of the story. It is important to note that the angel held the scroll in his *"hand"*. In verse 5 we are told that the angel lifted his *"hand"* toward heaven and **"sware that there should be time no longer." – Hebrewtoday.com**

Notes:_____

_____

_____

_____

_____

_____

_____

_____

THREE UNIVERSAL LANGUAGES

There are 3 universal languages: Mathematics, Music, and Biblical Hebrew.

The world was created using the twenty-two letters of the Hebrew alphabet

Yahweh confused the languages at Babel. All languages have their root in BIBLICAL HEBREW.

According to the Kabbalists the 22 letters are divided into 3 groups: the 3 Mother Letters, the 7 Double letters and the 12 Simple Letters. Do any of the other 22 related phenomena also divide naturally into this 3:7:12 pattern? If so then we have a stronger possible link between the Hebrew Alphabet and the other phenomena. In other words the fact that 2 sets of phenomena share not only the same overall number but also an inner pattern strengthens the case that they are linked.

Aleph, Shin and Mem

The Three Mother Letters

Shin = Fire
Aleph = Air
Mem = Water

Heaven was produced from Fire, The earth from Water, and Air from the Spirit.

In Music 3 notes make a chord, the major scale has 7 pitches and there are 12 notes in an octave. There it is again, that 3-7-12 pattern!

There are seven double letters in Hebrew:

The Seven Double Letters

Beth =	Aleph + Shin = Life
Gemel =	Aleph + Mem= Peace
Dalet =	Shin + Mem= Wisdom
Koph =	Beth + Gemel =Riches
Peh =	Beth + Dalet =Grace
Resh =	Dalet + Gemel = Fertility
Tau =	Aleph + Shin + Mem = Tav

They are called double letters because each letter presents a contrast: Life and Death, Peace and War, Wisdom and Folly, Riches and Poverty, Grace and Indignation, Fertility and Solitude, Power and Servitude.

The Seven Double letters produced the planets, the days of the week, and the Gates of the Soul (Our orifices of perception). From these seven came the Seven Heavens, the Seven Earths, and the Seven Sabbaths. Yahweh loved the number seven more than all things under Heaven.

The Twelve Simple Letters

Heh =	Aleph + Koph	= Sight
Vav =	Aleph + Peh	= Hearing
Zain =	Aleph + Resh	= Smell

Chet =	Aleph + Tau	= Speech
Tet =	Shin + Koph	= Taste
YOD =	Shin + Peh	= Sexual Love
Lamed =	Shin + Resh	= Work
Nun =	Shin + Tau	= Movement
Samekh =	Mem + Koph	= Anger
Ayin =	Mem + Peh	= Happiness
Tzaddi =	Mem + Resh	= Imagination
Qof =	Mem + Tau	= Sleep

The twelve Simple letters formed the twelve months of the year, the twelve organs (2 hands, 2 feet, 2 kidneys, the spleen, the liver, the gall, the bladder, sexual organs, the stomach and the intestines.)

Music, Colors and Time

According to the book of Job, The STARS SING!

Torah was originally sung! Angels have been known for singing from the very beginning. Ezekiel 28:11 says Lucifer was adorned with a beautiful voice. He led the heavenly choir.

Visually there are 3 primary colors...red, green and blue

In Calendar time there are 3 periods... A day, A month and A Year.

A coincidence noteworthy of mentioning regarding the first letters in the Hebrew names for the primary colors R(ed), G(reen) and B(lue). These 3 colors create all hues within the human visible spectrum.

The First letters in the Hebrew names for these colors span the distance of the Hebrew alphabet.

Aleph = Adom (RED)

Near the middle, the 10th letter is YOD

YOD= Yerakon (GREEN)

And at the end TAV. (Annotated)

THE HIDDEN PLURAL OF YOD

YOD is the 10th letter of the Hebrew alphabet, which gives it a numerical value of 10. Hidden in the word YOD is not only 10, but 20!

YOD represents HAND but Yahweh created human beings to have 2 hands.

YOD is spelled – YOD, VAV, DALET.

YOD is 10 + Vav is 6 + Dalet is 4 = 20. We have 2 hands for which to serve Yahweh. Or could it be that it's the "good" and the "bad"

The "good" and "bad" combination or comparison appears in the Bible 32 times!

Genesis 2:9, 3:5, 24:50, 31:24

Numbers 13: 19

Leviticus 27:10, 12, 14, 33

Deuteronomy 1:39

2 Samuel 13:22, 14: 17, 19:36

1 Kings 3:9

Isaiah 5:20

Jeremiah 42:6

Amos 5:14, 15

Micah 3:2

Psalms 31:12, 34:15, 37:27, 52:5

Proverbs 15:3, 31:12

Job 30:26

Lamentations 3:38

Ecclesiastes 12:14

2 Chronicles 18:17

From the very beginning mankind has been in search of the knowledge of "good" and "bad"-Which the eating of the tree of knowledge is supposed to help discriminate between.

"Good" and "bad" both refer to Yahweh's requirements. Is this true or false? Is this good or evil? Is this fact or fantasy? Truth or a lie?

Knowledge implies acquaintance with Yahweh's requirements who has laid down ordinances of Heaven and Earth. (Jer 33:25)

The regular sense of knowledge as commonly used today is about the world's specifications and requirements. What the world defines as "good" and "bad".

The code of human moral conduct fluctuates and changes with the times and seasons.

The first definition is about being able to tell the "good" from the "bad" as a result of being familiar with Yahweh's laws of human moral conduct. **There are 13 features of divine conduct as enumerated by Moses in Exodus 34: 6-7.**

"And the LORD passed by before him and proclaimed. THE LORD, THE LORD GOD, MERCIFUL AND GRACIOUS, LONGSUFFERING AND ABUNDANT IN GOODNESS AND TRUTH. KEEPING MERCY FOR THOUSANDS, FORGIVING INIQUITY AND TRANGRESSION AND SIN, AND THAT WILL BY NO MEANS CLEAR THE GUILTY VISITING THE INIQUITY OF THE FATHERS UPON THE CHILDREN AND UPON THE CHILDREN'S CHILDREN, UNTO THE THIRD AND TO THE FOURTH GERNERATION.

This is Yahweh's character!

The Bible repeatedly warns of the punishments awaiting violations of the divine moral requirements laid down by Yahweh. **(Annotated)**

THE MORAL LIFE

Out of the many admonishments that are explicitly expressed, it is clear to see that living a Holy life in the eyes of Yahweh is your life. The most important thing is to be "holy in His sight".

Notes:_____

_____

_____

_____

_____

_____

_____

_____

_____

"Take fast hold of instruction, let her not go; keep her, for she is thy life" – Proverbs 4:13

Since YOD is the number 10, let us look at the 10 areas of human moral life that we MUST pay close attention to and guard.

1. Imitation of God

2. Brotherly Love

3. Humility

4. Charity

5. Honesty

6. Forgiveness

7. Temperance

8. Duty to animals

9. Care of the Body

10. Rules of Health.

This is our obligation before Yahweh for HE IS OUR GOD!

CHAPTER 4

KAF

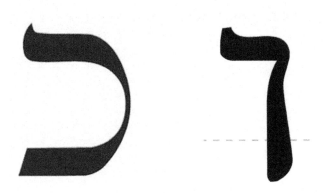

KAF is the eleventh letter of the Hebrew alphabet

Numerical value: 20

Sound: "K" with a **dagesh** (dot) and "KH" without a dagesh

Meaning: Palm, spoon, crown

The letter KAF is the first of five Hebrew letters that can be written in two forms. The first form ⤳ is used when KAF is at the beginning or in the middle of a word. The "final form" ⤳ is used when KAF is placed at the end of a word. **The letter KAF speaks of laying on of hands.** In both the old testament hands were laid on the animals before they were sacrificed. Joshua was ordained by the laying on of hands by Moses in Numbers 27:15, Deut 34:9 In the new testament, the Apostle Paul speaks of laying on hand in Timothy 4:14 and the laying on of hands was used to confer authority of designation of a person to a position of responsibility. Acts 6:6, Acts 13:3. Also the laying on of hands was associated with the receiving of the Holy Spirit. Acts 8:14-19

The first form of KAF assumes a "Kneeling position" and the "final form" of KAF appears to have a "standing position". It is said that the first for of KAF represent the humility of a believer during this life and the final form of KAF shows the believer stand in his glory before Yahweh in the end time. The "Final Forms" are prophetic of the "end of days". There are five letters that use "final forms" sometimes called "Sofit."

KAF

Mem

Nun

Pei

Tzaddi

We will cover each of these letters and their final forms with the chapter corresponding to that letter.

KAF has a numerical value of 20. It is said to be the "Symbol of crowning accomplishments." It is the first letter of the Hebrew word for "crown" = **"Keter." - chabad.org (Annotated)**

THE FOUR CROWNS

- **The crown of Priesthood**

- **The Crown of Kingship**

- **The Crown of Torah**

But the 4th crown, **the Crown of a Good Name** is superior to them all. – Jewish tradition

The letter *KAF* is bent. It represents a **כַּף יָד** *(KAF yad)* **palm of a hand**, like its name – *KAF*. It is shaped like a vessel that could hold and accommodate things within it. Therefore, people who have the letter *KAF* in their name are said to be ones who can handle the difficult things in their life and know how to accommodate other people. They are people with good managerial skills and who also possess strong financial capabilities. The curved, bent quality of the letter, also teaches that a person needs to be ready to bend themselves in modesty and to be accepting of others.

You may have noticed that the ram's horn blown on the Jewish New Year is also bent and curved, a sign that we must be humble and bend before the Master of the World.

As we mentioned the letter *KAF* represents the palm. When the Sabbath ends, there is a short religious ceremony called **הַבְדָּלָה** *(havdalah)*. This ceremony separates between the holy day of Sabbath and the ordinary weekdays. The *havdalah* includes three blessings, the third of which, involves using a candle. This blessing involves thanking Yahweh for fire. There is a custom to stretch one's palms towards the light of the candle and to open and close them. This is as if to say that the open hand represents the calm and restfulness of Sabbath, and the closed hand represents the hard work of the week. We are preparing to leave the restfulness and return to the busy world of work.

The final form of KAF (when it appears at the end of a word). It is not bent, but rather vertical and stands straight. This symbolizes the person who humbles and bends himself for his friends, and then, in the end, he will get respect for this and become upright and vertical.

And, finally, in the Bible, there are a few select places in which there are small letters. Like the KAF in the following verse: "לְשָׂרָה לִסְפֹּד אַבְרָהָם וַיָּבֹא תָהֹכִּלְבְ" (vayavo Avraham lispod le'Sarah velivekotah)…and Abraham came to mourn for Sarah, and to weep for her (Genesis 23:2). The commentators say that the small KAF indicates that Abraham held back his crying over Sarah. This was because he knew that she would merit greatness in the world to come, and therefore, didn't publicize his pain, and so to those around him, his grief appeared small.

The *gematria* of KAF is twenty. Twenty can be divided into ten and ten. The first ten represents the Ten Utterances with which God created the world. The second ten represents the Ten Commandments. Together, they become a KAF. In *Number* it states: "Ten-ten is the KAF."

If you take the word עשרים (esrim, the word "twenty" in Hebrew) and add up its letters, you arrive at 620: ayin=70, shin=300, reish=200, yud=10, mem=40. 620 is also the gematria of the word כתר, kesser: KAF=20, tav=400, reish=200. *Kesser* means crown, the ornament placed on the head of a king. *Kesser* also reminds us of the 620 letters in the Ten Commandments. God crowned the Jewish nation by giving them the Torah. And it became the Jews' **raison d'être** (most important reason), follow the 613 commandments and the 7 Rabbinic laws —**which together total 620**. Significantly, the first letter of *kisser* is KAF.

In *Kabbalah*, the *Sefirah* (or faculty) of *Kesser* represents a level that is beyond intellect. The crown is placed atop the head. Of course, our head is the vessel that carries the brain, the seat of intellect and thought. But the crown rests *above* the head, **beyond thought**. What can be greater than intellect? **Desire.** In Hebrew, this is called *ratzon*. Desire is a mighty force, inviting us to explore possibilities that rationality would show to be wrong or difficult. **(Annotated)**

Say, for example, you'd like to become successful in a particular occupation. Even though you may have failed every class in school, you can persevere and succeed if you have the will and desire. Why? Because you want to. The power, the crown, of desire is so potent that it has the ability to transcend and actually transform your intellect.

WHEN YOU REALLY WANT TO DO SOMETHING YOU CAN ACCOMPLISH THE UNEXPECTED OR IMPOSSIBLE.

On the other hand, there's another concept that even transcends desire, and that is pleasure (tainug). If a person derives pleasure from something he will automatically gravitate toward it. As a result he will mobilize his intellect and devise a strategy to attain it. That's why *kisser* is represented by the letter KAF—twenty—to teach us that there are two levels, or faculties, within the crown: desire and pleasure, with each faculty containing ten aspects. These aspects are also known as the **ten holy *Sefiros*** (spheres), **the ten building blocks of Creation**. Three of the ten levels reside in the dimension of the intellect—Wisdom, Understanding, and Knowledge—and seven occupy the dimension of the emotions—**Love, Fear, Mercy, Victory, Praise (Acknowledgment), Foundation (Bonding), and Sovereignty (Speech).** The two faculties of the crown of KAF—**pleasure and desire**—twice encompass the three levels of intellect and seven levels of emotion for a total of twenty levels.

It states in the *Talmud* that the crown of Torah is *halachah*—law. Why is it specifically law (i.e., those things that we should and shouldn't do) that is considered the crown of Torah? For the answer we can look to the reason God gave us the Torah. We did not receive the Torah to have some nice stories to entertain ourselves with, to read to our kids as a bedtime story, or to analyze in a literature class. On the contrary, the purpose of Torah is that we carry out His law, i.e., that we fulfill God's desire and in so doing give Him pleasure.

It therefore states in the *Talmud*: "Great is the study of Torah, for it brings one to action." Like the crown, Torah's ultimate purpose is to go beyond the head, beyond the intellect, and propel us to act in accordance with God's will, thereby refining us as people and completing God's purpose in Creation. – **(Annotated)**

MEANING

One of the meanings of the letter *KAF* is "spoon." The root of the word "spoon" is *KAFaf*—to bend. As we discussed earlier, the *KAF* is a letter that is bent. It represents the aspect of submitting oneself to a greater power. THAT GREATER POWER IS GOD! WE BEND TO SUBMIT OURSELVES TO GOD.

This notion of submission—and humility—can be seen clearly in the difference between the words *anochi* and *ani*. Both mean "I." When a person walks around all day and says, "I, I, I," he has a problem with egotism. How does one overcome this self-inflation? By adding a **KAF** to the אני (*ani*), the I, and transforming it into the אנכי (*anochi*). When the "I" submits to God, when it recognizes and bends to the higher power through the *KAF*, it is no longer the egotistical I. Rather, אנכי (*anochi*) is the "I" that serves as a channel to do God's will.

There are actually two *KAFs*. There's the bent *KAF* (כ), and the straight, or final, *KAF* (ך). What's the difference?

We explained previously that *Kesser*, the king's crown, is comprised of two levels: **pleasure and desire**. It has also been described as representing the internal and external aspects of the king. In this case, internal refers to the king's relation to himself, while external is his relationship to the world, his kingdom. Regarding the king's internal aspect—he doesn't necessarily want to be king, to be under the thumb of the ceaseless demands of his position. He wants to live within the boundaries of his own will, the internal world of study, erudition (The quality of having or showing great knowledge or learning) spirituality, and family. This is the meaning of the passage "From his shoulders up he was taller than the rest of his people," when speaking of King Saul, that is that he desired to be secluded from the people.

The king's crown, however, also demands the straight *KAF*, which unfurls to reach down to his subjects; the external level of the king's existence. He's required to interact, to be responsible and benevolent to his kingdom.

The bent *KAF* is a picture of the introverted or inverted king—who remains isolated within his internalized world. The straight *KAF* (similar to the *vav*) represents the king who descends from his high level and reaches down to others in order to communicate with and rule his people. This is also the position and mindset of each and every one of us. Internally we desire to live our lives on a level where we can be within our own will of serving God, living a peaceful life and enjoying our family. On the outside though, we must work and interact with society and maintain a certain amount of responsibility. The internal and external.

Interestingly enough, we observe that when you affix the straight *KAF* as the suffix to a word, it adds the word "you" to the root. As it says: "I will exalt *You* (ארוממך) my God the King." When you speak directly to a person, you say "you": *lecha,* לך, or *becha,* בך—spelled with a straight KAF: The final *KAF* thus *literally* unfolds to include the person to whom you are speaking. It represents the fact that the king has appeared to us and we are able to speak to him face to face. **Hebrewtoday.com (Annotated)**

Notes:_____

_____

_____

_____

_____

_____

The letter *KAF*. To bend oneself. To submit to the crown—the King, God, the ruler of the universe. Have you submitted yourself to the King of the Universe?

Notes:_____

_____

_____

_____

_____

_____

_____

_____

_____

_____

_____

_____

_____

_____

CHAPTER 5

LAMED

The twelfth **letter** of the **Hebrew** alphabet is called "**Lamed**" (pronounced "lah-med") and has the sound of "l" as in "look."

Lamed is the twelfth letter of the Hebrew alphabet

Numerical value: 30

Sound: "L"

Meaning: 1. Learn 2. Teach

Design

The twelfth letter of the *alef-beit* is the *lamed*. The design of the *lamed* is two letters merged together: the *vav* and the *KAF*. The *Kabbalah* says that the letter *lamed* is compared to **a tower flying in the air**. Why?

Gematria

The *gematria* of *lamed* is thirty. It states in *Ethics of Our Fathers*: "When one reaches the age of thirty, he reaches the age of full strength." We find in the *Torah* that when the Jewish people were in the desert, the *Levites* who carried the heavy vessels had to be between the ages of thirty to fifty, for these are the mightiest years of man. -Hebrewtoday.org

What was the reason why the Jewish people had to wander in the wilderness for forty years? The Bible tells us that it was the result of the sin of the Spies. Because the spies toured the land for 40 days and Israel didn't believe God enough to go in and take Jericho, GOD didn't like that and decreed the to remain in the desert for forty years. But why did they have to *wander* throughout the entire desert? Why not stay in one place going around and around in a circle? Why not set up camp and stay there for forty years. What was the reason for having to travel for a total of forty-two different journeys in forty years? Forty-two should ring a bell. Remember that Yahshua came down thru 42 generations from Abraham. Numbers are so significant in God's word and nothing is by chance. We remember seeing in the TET how the scriptures that held the secret of the letter was in Revelation 9 and the torment of man was in Revelation 9:19. This is not by happenstance but deliberate by design.

The purpose was to change the desert to a garden. By carrying the Ark of the Covenant with the Torah inside, each camp became a place of sanctity and peace. This is a lesson and for all of us that are walking with God. GOD is informing us that throughout our lives, we will have to travel. We will journey from country to country to and place to place. But wherever you go, you must take the Ark of GOD with you—ushering Godliness' to that area, elevating it and making its inhabitants more refined and spiritual. This is the purpose of a Jew. **(Annotated)**

This power to begin transforming the world in earnest begins when we turn thirty. THIS IS THE TIKKUN MENTIONED EARLIER. Up until that point we are in training. The *Midrash Shmuel* states that one has the ability to guide and influence others for good at the age of thirty. Until then, he is simply laying his foundation.

We find another interesting *gematria* in relation to *lamed*. Both the *alef* (in the form of the word *ulfana*) and the *lamed* (as in *lameid*) represent GOD as a teacher. What's the connection between the two letters? The design of the *alef* is comprised of two *yuds* and a *vav*: 10 and 10 and 6=26. The *lamed* is comprised of a KAF and a *vav*: 20 and 6=26. Twenty-six is the *gematria* of GOD's name, the Tetragrammaton *Yud-Hei-Vav-Hei*. *We covered this in Aleph in The Wonderful Hebrew Alphabet 1 workbook. So we are introduced to it again in Lamed as we begin to see Yahweh as a teacher.*

Yet there is a difference to be noted here between the teaching styles of the *alef* and the *lamed*. The *alef* is more theoretical while the *lamed* is more practical. Therefore the Alef resents the Written Law of Torah (stories and general concepts) while the *lamed* represents the Oral Law (how to practically apply these concepts in one's day-to-day life).

In another source, the *Rebbe* writes that the KAF of the *lamed* represents the human being, which is comprised of a GODLY soul and animal soul, each of which is comprised of ten faculties (equaling twenty). The *vav* represents GOD dwelling between them. The numerical value of the KAF is twenty. When GOD dwells between them, He adds His Ten *Sefiros*, or GODly energies, making thirty, which is *lamed*. - Hebrewtoday.org

Let's look at these faculties of the Godly Soul and the animal soul.

They are subdivided into two categories.

1. Three Intellectual Powers- These act thru the brain where they extend to the heart. From the brain they extend to other bodily organs thru the nervous system and manifest themselves thru various skills and arts performed by the body parts.

The Intellect has three faculties: CHOCHMAH,(Wisdom) BINAH (Understanding) AND DA'AT (Knowledge) - (ABBREVIATED AS CHaBaD)

2. Seven Emotional Powers – Chesed (Kindness), Gevurah (Severity in the sense of restraint) and Tiferet (Beauty such as in harmony) Netzach (Victory), Hod (Splendor), Yesod (foundation) and the seventh is Malchut (Majesty) through with all emotions are communicated.

IN ADDITION TO THESE TEN POWERS THE DIVINE SOUL POSSESSES THREE OUTLETS FOR CREATIVITY: THOUGHT, SPEECH AND ACTION!

MADE IN THE IMAGE OF GOD

This is what is meant by man being made in the image of God. We are created with the Divine or Godly soul qualities. Wisdom, understanding, knowledge, kindness, restraint, beauty, victory, splendor, foundation and majesty!

The animal soul has within it the Yetzar hara, the evil inclination. Although it is not necessarily "bad", it means contrary to Torah. Not living in a way of keeping the Torah and the commandments. So what is, "good?" Living in the way of Torah and keeping the commandments. If someone is hungry, the animal soul moves into motion to get food. If there is an obstacle in the way of food, the animal soul is sophisticated enough to get food in a way that is completely inventive. But the Yetzar Tov (the good inclination) always has the ability and potential to overcome the evil inclination. The animal soul also has two categories called Kelipot and literally means "shells" or "peels". Just as a shell covers fruit so the forces of Kelipah (Plural Kelipot) conceal Godliness. There are also three unclean Kelipot. The first category of Kelipotis called kelpat nogah (inclusive of light). This category contains; some measure of good. It is an intermediary level between good and evil. Therefore whatever receives its strength and vitality from this kelipah can be utilized for either good or evil. The second category consisting of the three impure kelipot is completely and wholly evil. Whatever receives it strength and vitality from this kelipah cannot be transformed into holiness or used in the service of God. These consist of ten "crowns" (as called in Kabbalistic terminology) of impurity. These ten faculties are: seven evil emotional traits These are lust, opposite of kindness, anger opposite of severity, boastfulness opposite of beauty and so forth. Whatever does not belong to the realm of holiness is "sitra achara" (literally the other side), not the side of holiness.

So let's break this down. The Apostle Paul said it best in Galatians 5:19-21 "Now the works of the flesh are manifest, which are these, Sexual immorality, imourity and debauchery, idolatry, witchcraft, hatred, discord, jealousy, fits of rage, selfish ambition, dissensions, factions and envy, seditions, murders, drunkenness, orgies and the like of which I tell you before, as I have also told you in time past, that they which do such things shall not inherit the kingdom of God. But the fruit of the Spirit is love, joy, peace, forbearance, kindness, goodness, faithfulness, gentleness, and self-control. Against such things there is no law. THOSE WHO BELONG TO CHRIST JESUS HAVE CRUCIFIED THE FLESH WITH ITS PASSIONS AND DESIRES. Since we live by the Spirit, let us keep in step with the Spirit." -NIV

GOD DWELLS ONLY IN THAT WHICH IS SURRENDERED TO HIM

Anything that does not surrender itself to God but considers itself as if it is a thing separate does not receive it's life from the holiness of God. Put another way, when someone determines that they do not need God and then does not surrender then their life power is not from God's holiness but from Satan who is the destroyer and that life leads to destruction. "For the thief comes to steal, kill and destroy, but I have come that you might have life and have it abundantly" John 10:10

What is the Kingdom of God? Yahshuah answered this question in Luke 17:21 when He said "the Kingdom of God is within you." A Kingdom is where a King rules. A government system. In saying that the Kingdom of God is within you, Yahshuah was clearly stating that. It is when God is ruling and governing YOU!

MAN WILL BE TESTED EVERYDAY UNTIL THE DAY HE DIES. THE LEVEL OF THOSE TESTS DEPEND ON THE SOPHISTICATION OF THE PERSON.

Back to the LAMED. The *Zohar* calls the *lamed* a tower flying in the air. The *vav* of the *lamed* represents GODliness, spirituality, found high up "in the air." The *vav*, which is a chute, draws this GODliness down from the spiritual realms into the physical world, until it is internalized into the KAF, the human being. This merging of spiritual and physical imbues the *lamed* with the ability to teach very lofty concepts in a practical way. - **chabad.org (Annotated)**

MEANING

Lamed means to learn and to teach—found in the daily prayers with the phrase *lilmod u'lameid.* But the word *lamed*, the commandment to teach, is not directed merely toward schoolteachers, it is a directive for *every* individual. **Every person can influence his or her friend or student, and every parent has the obligation to teach his or her children the knowledge of GOD, good deeds and ethics.** The Torah tells us that "You shall teach your children and talk to them about these things" (i.e., the Torah's commandments and responsibilities). The *Rambam* informs us that this passage is the premise for the *mitzvah* of *Talmud Torah*, Torah study; that through the commandment to teach our children, we know of our own obligation to study the Torah. For how can we teach our children the Torah if we haven't learned it ourselves?

THE COMMANDMENT TO TEACH YOUR CHILDREN WILL KEEP YOU IN STUDY

We can all ask a simple question: Why do we have to learn about this most essential commandment indirectly? If GOD wanted to tell us that we are obligated to learn Torah, why didn't He just say, "Learn Torah!" Why do we have to learn about this *mitzvah* by way of the commandment "Teach your children?"

The Rebbe explains that when it comes to studying Torah, a person **is *always* a child,** and thus the commandment to "teach your children" can also apply to us. One should never say, "Oh, I'm fifty now. I've read through the Torah more than twenty times. You can't teach me anything new." On the contrary, Torah is infinite. No matter how many times we have read it, studied it or learned it, we can always discover a new insight or uncover deeper meanings. We must approach it like children and be ready to receive and listen. As it states in *Ethics* *of Our Fathers:* "Who is wise? One who learns from everyone." "Everyone" can mean even someone who's younger than you. Even your children. Yahshuah said unless we come as children we cannot enter into the Kingdom of God. Matthew 18:3

This letter is the tallest letter of the Hebrew alphabet. Since it stands taller than all the other letters, it represents royalty. In fact, it represents the King of all kings, the Almighty.

The number 30, as represented by the LAMED, signifies the number of days in a full month according to the Jewish calendar.

It also represents the לֵב (*lev*) **heart**, as it is located in the center of the Hebrew alphabet.

The name of the letter – לָמֶד (*lamed*) – refers to לִימוּדִים (*limudim*) **studies**, or **learning**, which is the thing that most elevates people. Thanks to learning, a person's spiritual level rises and soars and they understand the meaning of creation.

The name of the letter לָמֶד(*lamed*) comes from its shape – מַלְמַד הַבָּקָר (*malmad habakar*) **cattle prod** or a **shepherd's staff**. *Malmad habakar* was a tool used in Biblical times. It was a piece of wood that was shaped like the letter *lamed*. The shepherd or farmer used it to direct his animals, as if he was מְלַמֵד (*melamed*) **teaching** the animals the correct way to go.

Lamed is special in more than just its appearance and its common usage within words. As with many letters of the Hebrew alphabet, it also stands as a preposition when used as a pre-fix. The letter *lamed* represents "to" and "for" – as in giving something to the woman or doing something for the man. It is also used when discussing a location to which something or someone is heading.

Another unique *lamed* role is its use to signal the infinitive form. Every Hebrew verbs's most basic conjugation is its infinitive form (e.g. to speak, to act, to write), and every infinitive in Hebrew starts with the letter *lamed*.

In the Book of Ecclesiastes (3:1-8), there is a list of activities that a person does at different times:

א

עֵת לָלֶדֶת וְעֵת לָמוּת עֵת . לַכֹּל זְמָן וְעֵת לְכָל-חֵפֶץ תַּחַת הַשָּׁמָיִםב.
לָטַעַת וְעֵת לַעֲקוֹר נָטוּעַ

עֵת לַהֲרוֹג וְעֵת לִרְפּוֹא עֵת לִפְרוֹץ וְעֵת לִבְנוֹת .ג

עֵת לִבְכּוֹת וְעֵת לִשְׂחוֹק עֵת סְפוֹד וְעֵת רְקוֹד .ד

עֵת לְהַשְׁלִיךְ אֲבָנִים וְעֵת כְּנוֹס אֲבָנִים עֵת לַחֲבוֹק וְעֵת לִרְחֹק מֵחַבֵּק .ה

עֵת לְבַקֵּשׁ וְעֵת לְאַבֵּד עֵת לִשְׁמוֹר וְעֵת לְהַשְׁלִיךְ .ו

עֵת לִקְרוֹעַ וְעֵת לִתְפּוֹר עֵת לַחֲשׁוֹת וְעֵת לְדַבֵּר .ז

עֵת לֶאֱהֹב וְעֵת לִשְׂנֹא עֵת מִלְחָמָה וְעֵת שָׁלוֹם .ח

1. To everything there is a season, and a time to every purpose under the heaven.

2. A time to be born, and a time to die, a time to plant, and a time to pluck up that which is planted;

3. A time to kill, and a time to heal; a time to break down, and a time to build up;

4. A time to weep, and a time to laugh; a time to mourn, and a time to dance;

5. A time to cast away stones, and a time to gather stones together; a time to embrace, and a time to refrain from embracing;

6. A time to seek, and a time to lose; a time to keep, and a time to cast away;

7. A time to rend, and a time to sew; a time to keep silence, and a time to speak;

8. A time to love, and a time to hate; a time for war, and a time for peace.

Take notice of the Hebrew language above , you'll see that all the verbs in these verses begin with the letter ל except for the verbs סְפוֹד (sefod) **mourn** and רְקוֹד (rekod) **dance.** The scholars understand from this that these two are different – they are both situations that remove a person from their learning – a funeral (when one is mourning) and a wedding (when one is dancing), which are both events that a person is obligated to go to, according to Jewish tradition.

It is also interesting to note that the O.T. ends (in the book of Chronicles) with the letter *lamed*. From this the commentators learn that someone who reads and studies the Bible reaches elevated spiritual levels, just like the *lamed* reaches upward.

The name יִשְׂרָאֵל (yisrael) **Israel** starts with the letter YOD, the smallest letter, and ends with the letter *lamed*, the tallest and biggest letter. This leads scholars to the idea that when individuals from the nation of Israel start to learn they are small, but when they finish learning, they are big and tall (spiritually, of course). Other scholars bring the interpretation that the nation of Israel will start out in a small, modest way, but when the End of Days comes, the nation will be higher than everyone else and will teach the other nations the divine truth. Yahweh has chosen Israel to bring the truth of the Torah to the world.

A person who has the letter *lamed* in their Hebrew name is one who enjoys a comfortable easy life. He or she is also someone who compromises easily, is creative, and enjoys art and music. This person is someone who has a strong desire to give a lot to others and doesn't ask much from them. **(Annotated)**

NUMBER

Thirty

- Thirty days of the month.

- Thirty-*shekel* value of an adult woman.

- Yahshuah was betrayed by Judas for 30 shekels of Silver

- The menstrual cycle.is every 30 days

- The thirty *tzadikim* in whose merit the world stands. Tzadikim are righteous ones.

- Thirty generations from Abraham to the destruction of the First Temple.

- Thirty levels of Kingship.

- Thirty categories of *tzadikim* in the World to Come.

FORM

A *vav* – whose head (*yud*) looks downward – on a KAF.

"A tower soaring in air."

The only letter ascending above the line.

- A three-stage rocket ship soaring into outer space.

- Man's aspiration to understand the universe.

- A heart of a wise man ascending to comprehend the wisdom of God.

- Learning in order to teach, learning in order to do.

- Divine inspiration; the higher *Shechinah*.

- Prophetic imagination breaking through the limitations of rational intellect.

-HEBREWTODAY.COM

Notes:_____

_____

_____

_____

_____

_____

_____

_____

_____

NAME

To learn; to teach. The power to direct and control the animal instinct.

- Learning secular skills; empirical knowledge.

- The yearning of the soul to learn Torah.

- Rectification of the power of imagination.

- Simultaneously learning in order to teach and learning in order to do.

Lamed, the ox goad, is intrinsically involved in both learning and teaching. Indeed, learning is the irritating process of being goaded into proper and productive action through the rigors of discipline. It is the process of being trained, so that one becomes accustomed to and comfortable with knowledge and understanding. It is the pain that brings the gain of a richer, fuller life in which one is positioned to act rather than constantly being acted upon. It is the bleeding that precedes the blessing, the drill that produces the thrill.

THIS IS THE SECRET OF LAMED

Yahshuah even emphasized the fact that the discipline of Christian discipleship is demanding and rigorous: *"And whoever does not bear his cross and come after Me cannot be My disciple... Whoever of you does not forsake all that he has cannot be My disciple"* (Luke 14:27, 14:33). God's *lamed* of discipline may well place demands of self-abnegation upon the disciple that will be painful; however, the rewards of yielding to the goad of discipleship produce the benefits of partnership with God and the blessings that accrue thereby.

Again, this is the core message of Christianity's Mega *Mitzvah* (Great Commission). *Yahshuah* instructed His talmidim in this manner: *"Go therefore and make disciples of all the nations... teaching them to observe all things that I have commanded you...*" (Matt. 28:19–20). The foundation of Christian discipleship is learning and teaching, and the foundation of the learning and teaching is the commandments of Yahshuah. Converts are made to the faith of *Yahshuah*, so that they may become disciples through the discipline of obedience to divine instructions. The fundamental meaning of the term that Yahshuah used to describe His followers sheds an entirely different light on the true nature of Christian discipleship. Christian discipleship is an exercise of learning through the discipline of instruction in Messiah's (Christ's) teaching. It is yielding oneself to the goad of training, permitting the pointed lamed to prick one's heart and marshal one's actions in the right and proper direction and to the God-determined end.

With the lamed imagery in focus, Yahshuah's invitation in Matthew 11:29–30 becomes much more clear and understandable: *"Take My yoke upon you and learn from Me..."* The metaphor is the same: Being yoked together with Yahshuah means learning—learning the teachings of Yahshuah, which are, after all, "easy." And one could just as readily say that *Yahshuah's lamed* (goad) is not cruel, inflicting unnecessary and excessive pain. It generates just enough discomfort to move the heart in the right direction of closer relationship with God and with one's fellow man.

THE ART OF LEARNING TO FOLLOW

Returning Christian discipleship to the matrix from which it was birthed brings greater understanding of both the concept and practice of discipleship. In the time of Messiah, discipleship was expressed in the teacher-student relationship. The dynamic exchange of knowledge, understanding, and wisdom that this relationship produced was and remains the essence of discipleship. The learning process was carried out in relationship, even apprenticeship, as it were.

The greatest honor of first-century Israel was to be "covered in the dust of the rabbi." How so? The learning process featured a "come walk the road with me" dynamic in which one followed the teacher and thereby was engaged in the great lessons of life in the course of everyday living. The rabbi-talmid (teacher-student) relationship was one of continual engagement, and the learning process was often one of imitation of practice more than an exchange of philosophical concepts. It was an exercise of following and learning by example. Classic examples that demonstrate the teaching-learning process produced by following are seen in the Moses-Joshua, Elijah-Elisha, and Paul-Timothy relationships. Joshua served as Moses's personal attendant and servant for decades before he was appointed to lead Israel. Perhaps the most important work that Elijah the prophet did occurred at the end of his career when he discipled Elisha and equipped him with the skills he would need for a "double portion" ministry. Paul carefully instructed Timothy in God's Word, so that he could replicate the apostle's vision, passion, and commitment in his own ministry. All of these disciples learned the lessons of life and ministry as they carefully followed their instructors. They walked with their teachers on a path that led to success.

And so it was with the disciples of *Yahshuah*. Those who had followed the

Master on the dusty roads of Israel were covered with dust, but not just the sandy granules of the Judean roadways. They were covered with the dust of His teaching—"*Yahshuah* dust," as it were. Others could tell that they had been with *Yahshuah*, not because of their words, but because of their actions (Acts 4:13). In following the Master, they had so conformed their lives to His actions that the Messiah now lived in and through them (John 14:23; Col. 1:27).

Following is more than a physical act. To be "Messiah-like" is to imitate the life of Yahshuah, keeping His commandments. When *Yahshuah* instructed His disciples to "follow" Him, He was asking them to commit themselves to a life of imitation in which they would mime the Master's actions. Those who followed *Rabbi Yahshuah* were able to give this instruction to others: "*Follow my example, as I follow the example of Messiah*" (1 Cor. 11:1). Their actions so imitated the life of Messiah that they became "Christians," dynamic models of the biblical lifestyle. For a true disciple, there is no greater pleasure or fulfillment than replicating the knowledge and actions of his teacher. This is the reward of intense observation, of insightful analysis, of unending rumination, of practical demonstration. Christian disciples faithfully replicate the life of the Messiah, their Master, as they follow in His footsteps. **(Hebrewtoday.com)**

LEARNING TO WALK WITH GOD

This idea of walking in fellowship with the Master and learning through the process is as old as humanity itself. God walked with Adam and Eve in the Garden of Eden, communicating to them His will for their lives. Later, Enoch walked with God in such a pleasing way that he was translated and did not experience death. Abraham walked with God and was perfect before his Maker because he walked in faith and faithfulness. He believed God, and he acted instantly and without reservation upon God's instructions. For this reason, God was not ashamed to be called the God of Abraham (Heb. 11:16).

Enoch's walk with God was of particular importance in that his very name in Hebrew, Hanoch, means "dedication" but with an emphasis on education. (The term *Hanukkah* comes from the same root and also means "dedication.") It has been suggested that Enoch was the first scientist, the first truly educated man. Because of his dedication to learn of God, Enoch pleased God and was received into God's presence supernaturally.

Micah spoke of the value of walking in dedication to God and gave his understanding as the summation of humanity's entire duty toward God: "*Do justly... love mercy, and... walk humbly with your God*" (Micah 6:8c). Doing right, seeking justice, rescuing the oppressed, defending the orphan, pleading for the widow—these things are the product of learning (Isa. 1:17). When one has so studied and learned divine instruction in the Holy Scriptures that he is able to conduct all of his affairs with justice and mercy, he has attained unto a position of walking humbly with God and is a true disciple.

John the apostle emphasized this kind of relationship: "*This is love, that we walk according to His commandments*" (2 John 6a). Paul fully agreed with this assessment: "*...We urge and exhort in the Lord Yahshuah that you should abound* *more and more, just as you received from us how you ought to walk and to please God"* (1 Thess. 4:1). Walking in obedient submission to God's instructions and commands is a walk of freedom (James 1:25). The prodding of the Holy Spirit will always turn the believer, who is so exercised, into the path of truth and justice, where there is, indeed, no condemnation. *- Hebrewtoday.com*

Notes:_____

_____

_____

_____

_____

_____

_____

_____

_____

_____

_____

_____

CHAPTER 6

MEM

Open Mem

Never used at the end of a word. Symbolic of an open womb.

Closed Mem

Only used at the end of a word. Symbolic of a closed womb.

Mem is the thirteenth letter of the Hebrew alphabet

Numerical value: 40

Sound: "M"

Meaning: 1. Water 2. Mashiach

Design

The letter *mem* is the thirteenth letter of the *alef-beit*.

There are two forms of the *mem*: the open *mem* and the closed *mem*. As the *Talmud* explains, the open *mem* represents the revealed *Torah* and the closed *mem* represents the Torah's secrets.

The *AriZal* states: "It is a *mitzvah* to reveal the secrets of Torah." Being that we now find ourselves in the Messianic era, it is not just permitted, it is an *obligation* to experience a foretaste of the teachings of <u>Mashiach</u>, which are the secrets of the Torah. This level of Torah is represented by the closed *mem*.

The *Rambam* begins his first book, the *Mishneh Torah*, with a section of laws entitled "The Foundations of Torah." In this section, he discusses *Yahweh*, the angels, and the heavens, and explains: "This that I told you up until now is called 'the secrets of Creation and the secrets of the Chariot." These mystical insights are complex Kabbalistic concepts. Yet the *Rambam* decided to teach them as a foundation—a prerequisite for everyone who studies the Torah. The apprehension of Yahweh's awesomeness, of His stirring and unfathomable ways, must precede even the essential laws of the revealed Torah, such as the *Shema*, Shabbat and *tefillin*.

Additionally, the *mem* represents the womb— רחם (*rechem*)—which ends with a closed *mem*. The closed *mem* represents the nine months when the womb is closed. The open *mem* represents the period of childbirth, when the womb is open.

Gematria

The *gematria* of *mem* is forty. Forty is the number of days it rained upon the earth during the Flood. Forty is also the number of days Moses spent on Mount Sinai. Moses actually ascended up the mountain three separate times. The first forty-day sojourn took place when he received the Torah. Then Moses descended with the Tablets but shattered them when he saw the Golden Calf that the people had made in his absence. The following morning Moses returned to the mountain for another forty days to pray on behalf of the Jewish people. When Moses returned to the encampment, Yahweh called out for him to return to the mountain, this time, with his own tablets. So Moses dug under his tent and found two sapphire stones. He brought them up with him to Mount Sinai for the third and final forty days, and Yahweh engraved the Ten Commandments on them. It was the tenth of the month of Tishrei when Moses came down from the mountain with Yahweh's law after these final forty days. Yahweh declared, "I have forgiven [the Jewish people] as you have asked." The culmination of these three forty-day periods, the tenth of Tishrei, Yom Kippur, is thus the day we as the Jewish people fast and pray to atone for our sins.

There are other significant references to forty in the Torah: Moses' spies scouted the land for forty days. The Jews were in the desert for forty years. And a *mikveh*, a ritual bath, is made up of forty *se'ah* (about 200 gallons).

What is the concept of forty? Forty represents a metamorphosis, a transformation. After forty days, the embryo of a child begins to assume a recognizable form.

Additionally, a *mikveh* (with its forty *se'ah*) has the ability to change an individual from a state of impurity to purity. And if one wants to undertake a conversion, one must immerse in a *mikveh*, whereupon his or her Jewish soul is revealed.

Yahweh brought a flood upon this world for forty days and forty nights. The waters of the flood were not for revenge, as is commonly assumed, but for atonement, to purify and transform the world, in much the same way a *mikveh* purifies a person.

Each of Moses' forty-day sojourns in heaven signified a transformation. The first forty days was to receive the Torah, and when an individual learns Torah, he or she develops the ability to change for the better. The second trip was for prayer, *tefillah*. When a person prays, he or she can change an evil decree; in this case, Yahweh's intention to annihilate the Jewish people. Indeed, because of Moses' supplications, Yahweh was willing to bestow His mercy and once again offer them His Torah. The final ascent represented *teshuvah* (repentance)—also a transformation—because once a person has repented, he is no longer the same person he was when he sinned. When Moses finally returned to the Jewish people with Yahweh's law, they were at a level of atonement—and thus finally prepared to become Yahweh's nation.

Furthermore, the words Torah, *tefillah* and *teshuvah* begin with a *tav*, which has the numerical value of 400, or 40x10 (i.e., serving Yahweh with all of one's 10 faculties for 40 days) - **Hebrewtoday.com**

Notes_____

_____

_____

_____

_____

_____

We are commanded to Love Yahweh with all our heart, our soul (mind) and our might. **The 10 faculties of the mind are**

1. **Consciousness**

2. **Imagination**

3. **Perception**

4. **Thinking**

5. **Intelligence**

6. **Judgement**

7. **Language**

8. **Memory**

9. **Emotion**

10. **Instinct.**

The forty years that the Jews spent in the desert also constituted a transformation. The nation that had rebelled against Yahweh had metamorphosed into a nation that was ready to adhere to His word.

MEANING

The word *mem* stands for *mayim*, which means water. Water constitutes a vital element in our lives: a human being is largely composed of water and the majority of the earth is covered with it.

Torah, the most vital element in our spiritual lives, is referred to as water, as it states: "Ein mayim ela Torah—There is no water but Torah." As the Prophet tells us, "He who is thirsty shall go and drink water," meaning that a Jew's thirst for spirituality will never be sated by looking to other cultures or religions. The only thing that will quench one's thirst is water, which is Torah.

Just as a fish cannot survive without water, a Jew cannot survive without Torah. The story is told of a fish and a fox. The fish was busy evading a fisherman's net when he spied a fox standing on the shore of the lake. The fox called out to the fish and said, "Little fish, where are you going?" The fish answered, "The fishermen are all trying catch me, so I'm trying to swim away!" Feigning concern, the conniving fox offered, "Little fish, come up out of the water. I will protect you." Replied the fish, "Silly fox. In the water I still have a chance. But once I leave the water, I will surely die."

A Jew without Torah is like a fish without water. Of course we know that the water isn't without its difficulties. There is anti-Semitism. We run from country to country, trying to survive a Spanish Inquisition and a Holocaust. Yet even amidst the onslaught, we have persevered as a people. The moment we leave our culture, the moment we leave the water—our connection to Yahweh and Torah—we are spiritually dead.

Torah is also compared to water because water travels unaltered from the top of a mountain to its lower tiers and valleys. So did Yahweh bring down the same deep, intellectual Torah He had in heaven to the physical world. The *Zohar* says that Yahweh looked into the Torah to create the world. The Torah serves as a blueprint for Creation. The wealth and strength of its water carves, and continues to carve out the foundation of the entire world.

The *Mishnah*, the Oral Law of Torah, begins and ends with the letter *mem*. Its first word is *M'eimasai* and its concluding word is *bashalom*, "peace." Furthermore, the *Rambam* also begins and ends his great work, the *Mishneh Torah*, with a *mem*—beginning the first chapter with the word *Meshoch*, and concluding the final volume with the word *mechasim*.

The *mem* also represents the womb. In essence, water is the womb of Creation. The Torah begins, "In the beginning Yahweh created the heavens and the earth." The next verse states that before Yahweh created the heavens and the earth "...the spirit of Yahweh hovered over the waters." What waters? Since the earth's waters had not yet been created, the waters mentioned here are the womb from which Creation emerged, the place of gestation before the world came into existence.

Mikveh embodies this concept as well. When one immerses in a *mikveh*, it is similar to entering the womb of Creation, a state of the world yet unborn. At the moment when the person emerges, he or she is reborn. On a more practical level, the individual submerged in a *mikveh* is in a medium where he or she can't survive and will ultimately die. When the individual emerges from the water, he or she is renewed. The word *mikveh* also begins with the letter *mem*.

It states in Isaiah: "*L'marbei hamisra u'leshalom*," which means, "His rule (i.e., the kingship of Mashiach) will increase and be blessed with peace without end." Throughout the entire Torah, the final form of the *mem* appears in the middle of a word only once—here, in the word לםרבה, *l'marbei*. What is the significance of this? That *Mashiach* will bring closure to the exile. We discussed earlier that the three lines of the letter *beit*—two horizontal and one vertical—represent three directions (or corners) of the earth. The north side, that which is open to evil, remains unresolved. With the arrival of *Mashiach*, the fourth side of the *beit* of *Bereishis*—Creation—is completed and the letter *beit* is transformed into a *mem*. And the emergence of this form of the *mem* in turn facilitates the consummation of its very own design, whereby the closed *mem*—the hidden or secret aspects of Torah—takes the place of the open *mem*, the revealed aspects of the Torah. For along with the everlasting peace of *Mashiach* will come the explanation of the reasons for the exile, and the pain and suffering of the Jewish people that accompanied it. - **CHABAD.ORG**

Let's look at Mem on another level

MEM IS THE HALF-WAY MARK THRU THE LETTERS OF THE ALEPH-BEIT.

The open MEM indicates the revealed – everything that we see in creation and understand in the simplest way.

The final letter form ם is completely closed on four sides, and it symbolizes the parts of creation that we cannot understand.

One of the names of Yahweh is – מָקוֹם (makom) which literally means **place**. This name expresses that the presence of Yahweh exists in every place. It is interesting to see that the first letter of מָקוֹם is *mem*, and that the last letter is also a *mem*, in its final letter form. In the middle is the word קו (kav) **line**. It is as if this is a line between the known world and the hidden, not completely understood world.

Another name of Yahweh is – אֱמֶת (emet) which means **truth**. This word starts with the first letter of the Aleph-Bet – א – and ends with the last letter – ת. This refers to all of existence and the truth in it. The middle of the word is the letter מ which connects between the different worlds of creation, as we mentioned earlier.

Another word that starts and ends with the letter מ is the word מים. In the story of the Creation, the text mentions that Yahweh separated the waters above the firmament and below it. The first *mem* represents the waters above the firmament and the second *mem* the waters below the firmament.

Therefore this letter is connected to the element of water.

The numerical value of the letter מ is 40. This number represents ripeness and maturity. This is because according to Jewish tradition, 40 days after conception, a fetus begins to take on human form.

The ideal full life for a person is 120 years (based on the life of Moses), which splits into three segments of 40 years. Each segment is a stage of different stage development in a person's life.

The number also appears in many Biblical stories: Some were mentioned above but here are two more instances.

- Jonah the prophet told the people of Ninveh that they had 40 days to repent.

- The Children of Israel wandered in the desert for 40 years – the amount of time they needed to free themselves of the slave mentality and become an independent, free nation.

As we said, the letter n is connected to water, and the connection between the revealed and hidden worlds. This letter represents warm feelings, motherhood, and lots of love.

NUMBER

Forty

- Forty days of the flood.

- Forty *seah*, the minimum quantity of water required for a kosher *mikveh*.

- Forty years of wandering in the Desert.

- Forty days from conception to the initial "formation" of the fetus.

- "Forty less one":

- The punishment of stripes;

- The categories of work forbidden on the Sabbath;

- The weeks of pregnancy.

- Forty days of Israel waiting for Moses to descend with the Torah.

- The (three) forty-year periods in the lives of Moses and Rabbi Akiva.

- Forty generations from Moses to the completion of the Talmud

- Forty days of "lower *teshuvah*" for the sin of the Golden Calf. TESHUVAH IS RETURNING TO GOD.

- Forty days of "higher *teshuvah*" in which Moses received the second tablets.

- Forty cubits – the height of the entrance to the Sanctuary of the Temple.

The first time the letter mem appears in the Torah as the root of a word is in the first chapter of the Book of Genesis where the word mayim is used: ***"The earth*** *was without form and an empty waste, and darkness was upon the face of the very great deep. The Spirit of God was moving (hovering, brooding) over the face of the waters."* Genesis 1:2 AMP. Based on the law of first mentions, it can be said that water represents the Spirit of God. - **Hebrewtoday.com**

Thus, mem represents the Spirit of God: *As soon as Jesus was baptized, he went up out of the water. At that moment heaven was opened, and he saw the Spirit of God descending like a dove and lighting on him. And a voice from heaven said, "This is my Son, whom I love; with him I am well pleased." Matthew 3:16-17*

The word for love in Hebrew is אהבה ahavah and it has a numerical value of 13. The letter mem also speaks of the love of God.

CHAPTER 7

NUN

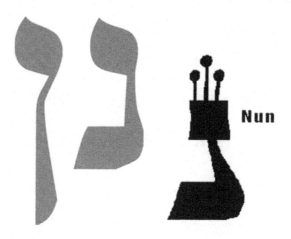

Nun

The Letter Nun (נ)

(Please note that the pronunciation of this letter is somewhere between nun and noon.)

This letter also has two different forms – the regular letter נ and the special final letter ן.

The letter *nun* represents giving. If we look at the word נָתַן (*natan*) **gave**, we see that it starts and ends with the letter נ. This teaches us the reciprocal nature of giving. When one gives to another person, it comes back to him/her in some way.

A person who has the letter *nun* in their name is someone who takes charge of his/her life and does not let things that happen get him/her down. However, the letter |ון (*nun*) can either sit in its place, like its shape נ, or it can stand like in its final letter form ן. Remember that when letters are in their final form they represent the end of time. In other words, the NUN is SITTING NOW, BUT WILL BE STANDING THEN.

This means that the willpower that is expressed in this letter, is something that changes from person to person, and can also change at different times. In fact, our actions can change the situation that we are in.

THE THINGS WE DO CAN TOTALLY CHANGE A SITUATION, FOR GOOD OR BAD!

Someone who has the letter נ in their name, is also a person who has great self-confidence, is knowledgeable, and is good at creating connections with his/her surroundings. However, he/she is not a person who is good at solving problems when they get stuck in a difficult situation, and this is liable to influence their mood. They are good at exact sciences and are talented in technical matters.

The numerical value of the letter נ is 50, and the Jewish sages say that 50 years old is the age of advice. This is an age when someone is wiser and knowledgeable and is able to give good advice to those around him.

|ון is actually the Aramaic word for fish, and has been incorporated into the Hebrew names of several marine creatures – such as דְיוֹנוּן (*dyonun*) **squid** and תְמָנוּן (*tmanun*) **octopus**. This teaches that this letter is also connected to the element of water.

The |ון also symbolizes the נְשָׁמה (*neshama*) **soul, spirit,** and the sages say that the number **50 represents both purity and impurity together**. Therefore, the soul is susceptible to both of these elements and people who have the letter in their name **must be careful to take the good parts of life and enrich their souls accordingly.**

If you look at chapter 145 in Psalms, you'll see that it is an acrostic and that the verses go according to the letters of the Aleph-Bet. Each letter appears at the beginning of a verse, except for the letter נ. Commentators say that the reason for this is that the letter also hints at נְפִילָה (nefila) downfall, and therefore King David, the composer of Psalms, left this letter out. In contrast to this, he emphasized the helping and saving aspects of GOD in the verse of the next letter, ס, with the words: "סוֹמֵךְ יְהוָה לְכָל-הַנֹּפְלִים" (somech hashem lechol hanoflim) **"The LORD upholdeth all that fall."** He thereby encourages us that the Almighty will help us in a situation where we fall. - (**Annotated**)

NUMBER

Fifty; the fifty gates of understanding.

- The cycle of fifty years culminating in the Jubilee year.

- "Fifty years to counsel."

- The fifty queries into the nature of Creation which God poses Job.

- Fifty references to the Exodus in Torah.

- Fifty images in Torah "supported" by the Name of God.

- Fifty days of counting the *Omer* between *Passover* and *Pentecost*

- Fifty thousand Jubilees of the World to Come.

THE MESSIAH – HEIR TO THE THRONE

In Aramaic, *nun* means "fish." The *mem* means the waters of the sea. Water is the natural medium of the *nun*, fish. The *nun* "swims" in the *mem*, covered by the waters of the "hidden world." Creatures of the "hidden world" lack self-consciousness. Land animals on the face of the earth possess self-consciousness. Earlier it was thought that goldfish had a memory of only three seconds long, which showed how gracious God was to them being they swim in a bowl all day long. With such a short memory it always looked like they were swimming somewhere new. Now scientists have proven that goldfish actually remember things for at least five months!

NUN is the 14th letter of the Hebrew Alphabet, and so the 7th of the second set of 7 letters and repeats the theme of our future or final REWARD, INHERITANCE, HEAVEN, day of REST, etc. The NUN particularly emphasizes the PROMISED INHERITANCE.

The number 153, which is the amount of fish caught by the Peter and the disciples in John 21:11, is also the gematria of the Hebrew phrase "the sons of God" (beney ha'elohim). The disciples would probably have known exactly the significance **of 153 fish** and "none being lost". 153 is also a "triangular" number. Triangular numbers are numbers that can make a triangle dot pattern.

153 is symbolic of "all the elect of God" or "sons of God".

NUN also means "promised seed"...so this may be another reason for the fish being a symbol used by the early church.

In the Bible, verses 35-36 in Numbers 10 are enclosed by two "up-side-down" letter NUNs. It is so written in the most ancient manuscripts and always copied as such in all temple scrolls. It takes a bit of study to come to a conclusion about the inverted NUNS, One answer is that they are scribal notations that the verse did not belong there. Another answer is that they actually enclose a separate 'BOOK' in themselves, so that we don't have 5 books by Moses, but seven. Personally I believe that more will be revealed about the inverted NUNS when Messiah comes. There are more inverted NUNS in Psalm 107.

Regarding the use of the fish as a symbol for the early church, "promised seed", all believers are Abraham's seed, because we are "in" Christ who is THE promised seed.

Galatians 3:29

The passage in numbers enclosed by the two NUNS is the prayer of Moses as the children of Israel moved about the wilderness:

Num 10:35-36 And it came to pass, when the ark set forward, that Moses said, Rise up, LORD, and let thine enemies be scattered; and let them that hate thee flee before thee. And when it rested, he said, Return, O LORD, unto the many thousands of Israel.

Other scriptures confirm that it was Christ himself who was with the children of Israel in the wilderness and so these" NUNS could very well be symbolic of the "promised seed, Christ" who "enclosed" or "CONTINUED" with them in the wilderness. He is called the "Angel of his Presence and the Rock:

Isa 63:9 In all their affliction he was afflicted, and the angel of his presence saved them: in his love and in his pity he redeemed them; and he bare them, and carried them all the days of old. 1Cr 10:1-5 Moreover, brethren, I would not that ye should be ignorant, how that all our fathers were under the cloud, and all passed through the sea.... And did all drink the same spiritual drink: for they drank of that spiritual Rock that followed them: and that Rock was Christ. But with many of them God was not well pleased: for they were overthrown in the wilderness.

Now, the Jews have always believed the Hebrew word "yinun or yinon" (sp. YOD/NUN/VAV/NUN) translated as "continue" in Ps. 72, is another name for the Messiah. The letter YOD means "hand or right hand" and NUN was also the name of the father of Joshua (the transliterated Hebrew name of Jesus), making "yinun" literally "the right hand of the Father" (of Yeshua). Yet another reason for the NUN or fish to be significant to the church.

Psa 72:17 His name shall endure forever: his name shall be continued (YINUN) as long as the sun: and [men] shall be blessed in him: all nations shall call him blessed.

NUN is used for the number 50, which in Hebrew is the year of the JUBILEE, the year when all INHERITANCE was returned to the original owner, fitting into the same symbolic significance.

The first word that begins with a NUN in the OT is "nefesh" which means "soul or creature, or any living thing". But here, in its FIRST use, it is speaking of FISH!

The *Maharal* explains that the two *nuns* represent the two fundamental approaches to serving GOD: fear and love. The first person serves GOD out of awe, fear. Therefore, he is hunched over. The second person serves GOD out of love and thus stands straight. This person is also characterized by generosity because love represents openness.

Another interpretation is found in the work of the *Shelah*, where it states that the bent *nun* alludes to one who has fallen and the straight *nun* to one who has straightened back up.

Rashi comments that if a person is "bent over" throughout his life, that means he is humble. He is subservient to law and order, to Torah and to GOD. In the World to Come he will stand tall and straight, for GOD will bless him with tremendous reward.

It is interesting to note that in a *halachic* debate, the final verdict in Jewish law isn't necessarily bestowed upon the one who is the more intelligent. Rather it is decided based on the opinion of the person who is the more humble. What does the Torah tell us about Moses? Not that he was a brilliant scholar, but that he was the epitome of humility.

The same is true of Joshua, Moses' successor. As some sources compare Moses to a fish, a *nun*, because he was taken out of the water by Pharaoh's daughter, so is Joshua called *"ben Nun,"* the son (disciple) of this great fish (Moses). Torah does not inform us about his intellect, but rather that he was Moses' disciple— that he was always at Moses' side and in Moses' tent. Why did he merit inheriting the leadership of the Jewish people from Moses? Because he embraced the quality of humility with his entire being.

Even before King David became king he was known as "the final verdict." King Saul, his predecessor, was brilliant, but the *halachah* was determined according to David. We know that David was very humble; he is called "the servant of the LORD" and "My servant David." Additionally, Hillel, the famous Tannaic rabbi and scholar, faced off time and time again against his colleague Shammai in determining Jewish law. Shammai was actually intellectually sharper than Hillel, but the *halachah* was decided according to Hillel because of his humility and kindness.

It states in the *HaYom Yom:* "The unique quality of *Mashiach* is that he will be humble. Though he will be the ultimate in greatness—for he will teach Torah to the Patriarchs and to Moses—so, too, he will be the ultimate in humility and self-nullification, for he will also teach simple folk."

Whether one serves GOD out of love or fear, or whether one is bent or straight, the spark of *Mashiach* found within all of us will empower us with the humility to embrace the diversity of creation. – **(Annotated)**

Gematria

The *gematria* of *nun* is fifty. There are fifty "gates" or levels of *Binah*. Binah is the attribute of understanding. That's why the Jews counted forty-nine days—seven complete weeks from Passover to Pentecost—to ready themselves to receive the Torah. The famous question is, why does the Torah tell us to count fifty days after Passover, when immediately afterwards it says to count seven complete weeks, which are only *forty-nine* days? The answer is that an individual can only attain forty-nine levels of intellect on his own. The fiftieth level, that of transcendence, can only be provided by GOD. Therefore, GOD says: You do yours and I will do Mine. If you achieve the forty-ninth level, I will bless you with the fiftieth; the highest tier of *Binah*, understanding.

On the Jewish calendar, every fiftieth year is called the year of *Yovel*, or Jubilee. In the Jubilee year, all lands in the Land of Israel are "given their freedom," and returned to their original owners. - **my Jewish learning**

How is the concept of freedom and the Torah connected? In *Ethics of Our Fathers* it states: "One who learns Torah is truly free," but for the skeptic to challenge this statement would be all too easy. *"Free?!* What do you mean free? The Torah is full of restrictions! It tells me not to do this and not to do that. Some freedom!"

Yet indeed, when one learns Torah, he is free of the false, materialistic constraints of society. Free from his self-centered, animalistic inclinations. He has the power to confront and transcend these obstacles. Furthermore, Torah gives an individual the ability to maximize his potential, to be the best he can be.

As an example, when you are eating good, nutritious food, your performance is optimally enhanced. Sure, you can survive on potato chips and soda pop, but not very healthy and not for very long. The fact of the matter is, when you eat healthful foods, you're able to produce better. You are properly fueling your vessel.

The same holds true regarding living according to the laws of Torah. Some people believe they don't need the Torah in their life, that they can survive very well without it. They believe since they have all the material amenities to live relatively stress-free and comfortable and their social life is in full swing. But when they *do* decide to live a Torah lifestyle, they soon realize that they are able to operate at a much higher plane of existence than the average individual. They feel that they are in control of their lives and are not enslaved to the dictates of the false values of society. - Hebrewtoday.com **(Annotated)**

Notes_____

_____

_____

_____

_____

_____

_____

_____

_____

Meanings

The *Zohar* tells us that the **_nun stands for ona'ah—deceit._** To the human eye, this world seems to be controlled by the laws of nature, because cannot see GOD. This false reality therefore is a total deception.

The mission for all of us is to reveal and draw GOD's infinite light down into this world, so that we can see the true reality of the world—that everything is GODliness and GODliness is everything. This is done by cleaving to GOD and observing His commandments. This concept is expressed in the straight, long (final) *nun*, which has a design similar to the *vav*, a chute. In contrast to the vav, however, its leg extends beneath the baseline. This implies the downward flow of Divine energy reaching into even the deepest abyss. This will ultimately happen with *Mashiach's* arrival.

Nun also means "kingship." There is a verse in *Tehillim* (Psalms), regarding *Mashiach* that states: "May his name (Yinon) endure forever, as long as the sun" According to *Rashi*, Yinon refers to kingship. If we break the word "Yinon" into two—*yud* and *nun*—*nun* means kingship, and putting a *yud* before a word denotes continuity. Therefore, the name Yinon implies that the kingship of *Mashiach* will endure forever.

In Aramaic, *nun* means a fish. **Another meaning of nun is a bar nafli, one who has fallen, or a miscarriage**. In the Torah portion entitled Balak, the prophet Bilaam prophesizes the coming of two kings. The first one is King David. The second is King *Mashiach*, who will rise from David's descendants in the final days.

The *Midrash* states **that David was originally supposed to have died through a miscarriage.** He was able to survive only because Adam (the first man) **bequeathed David seventy of his own years**. Therefore, Adam who **should have**

lived to be 1,000 yrs old died at 930 yrs old.

Mashiach, a descendant of David, is called a *bar nafli*, literally translated as the "son of one who has fallen," or a miscarriage. A miscarriage causes great pain and suffering to the mother and to those close to her. The role of pain and suffering is an important element of *Mashiach's* presence on earth. Because he feels the suffering of the Jewish people, he will pray fervently on their behalf to bring redemption and healing.

King David is known as David ben Yishai—the son of Yishai. It is interesting to note that the *gematria* of בן ישי, "ben Yishai," **is 372, the same value as the words** בר נפלי, **bar nafli. - MISCARRIAGE!**

The Talmud tells us there was a debate over the name of Mashiach. One group said the name of Mashiach is Menachem. The other group said it's Shiloh. The third group said Mashiach's name is Yinon. The fourth group said Chanina. In essence, they were all correct. Mashiach (spelled mem, shin, yud, chet) is an acronym of all four names. The mem of Mashiach represents Menachem, which means consolation, for Mashiach will come and console the Jewish people and soothe their pain and anguish from the exile and the destruction of the First and Second Holy Temples. Then he will be Shiloh (shin), which means he will become king and reign over the people, restoring law and order. Shiloh, which also means "gifts to him," refers to one's obligation to bring presents to the king. Then he will be Yinon (yud), which means fish that multiply rapidly and endure. Under Mashiach's reign, the world will be fruitful and multiply. The last name is Chanina (chet). Chanina means chein, grace. Mashiach will ultimately bring grace, peace, and harmony to the world.

Furthermore, the Talmud tells us that a person who dreams "and sees Chanina" is destined to witness "many, many" miracles, because there are two nuns in the word Chanina. The word nun also means nes, miracle. Two nuns denote nisei nissim: many, many miracles. In the era of Mashiach, everyone will witness great wonders and miracles.

In conclusion, *nun*, which represents humility, is the vessel for all of GOD's blessings. Intellectually, when one is humble, one acquires the fiftieth (and crowning) level of understanding; on a material level, one attains abundant material wealth through his ability to "multiply like a fish." Through our efforts to achieve humility, we will be blessed both materially and spiritually with the coming of *Mashiach*. - **Hebrewtoday.com (Annotated)**

Conclusion

This little book is packed with a world of knowledge that will change your life forever. Knowing the spiritual meaning of the letters of the Hebrew Alphabet which is God's language will open doors for you that you have never imagined, in this world and in the world to come. Embrace this with everything in you and get the revelation that Yahweh has for you. Begin to look at the world differently in connection to the letters and how the letters give the essence of what an object or person truly is. Brighter days are ahead. I hope you find this an endeavor that you will pursue for the rest of your life and devote yourself to lifelong exploration of the mystery of the Wonderful Hebrew Alphabet.

This concludes our study of the second set of letters. I pray you have been blessed and will continue to review this book regularly until you have gained a thorough understanding of the letters and their meanings. Remember, each letter is a WORD. Study the WORDS for the relevance to Yahshuah the Messiah.

Join us in the next book which will study the third set of letters in the ALEPH-BEIT.

SHALOM!

REFERENCES

In His Words by Grant Luton

Hebrew 4 Christians.com

My Jewish Learning.com

Chabad.org

Mysteries of the Menorah

Bridges for Peace

HebrewToday.com

Christian forums

Made in the USA
Coppell, TX
08 June 2021